KU-169-138

THE MURDER OF
MEREDITH
KERCHER

GARY C. KING

THE MURDER OF
MEREDITH KERCHER

GARY C. KING

JOHN BLAKE

Published by John Blake Publishing Ltd,
3 Bramber Court, 2 Bramber Road,
London W14 9PB, England

www.johnblakepublishing.co.uk

First published in paperback 2010

ISBN: 978 1 84454 902 3

All rights reserved. No part of this publication may be reproduced,
stored in a retrieval system, or in any form or by any means, without the
prior permission in writing of the publisher, nor be otherwise circulated in
any form of binding or cover other than that in which it is published
and without a similar condition including this condition
being imposed on the subsequent publisher.

British Library Cataloguing-in-Publication Data:
A catalogue record for this book is available from the British Library.

Design by www.envydesign.co.uk

Printed in Great Britain by CPI Bookmarque, Croydon CR0 4TD

1 3 5 7 9 10 8 6 4 2

© Text copyright Gary C. King 2010

Papers used by John Blake Publishing are natural, recyclable products made
from wood grown in sustainable forests. The manufacturing processes
conform to the environmental regulations of the country of origin.

All photographs © *Rex Features*

In memory of Meredith Kercher

Murder most foul, as in the best it is;
But this most foul, strange, and unnatural.

—William Shakespeare, *Hamlet*

ACKNOWLEDGEMENTS

A very special thanks to editor John Wordsworth at John Blake Publishing for wanting to do this book and for wanting to do it with me. He could have had his pick of any number of writers eager to do this story, but I am grateful he chose me. After reading my thrice-weekly blog on True Crime Report (www.truecrimereport.com), John asked me if I'd be interested in writing a book on the Meredith Kercher case. Naturally, who could say no? I enjoyed working with John on this project, without whose skills and enthusiasm this book would not have made if off the presses.

I am, of course, also very grateful to John Blake, publisher of John Blake Publishing, who was immediately keen on doing a book about this case even though he and his company had never worked with me before. He took a calculated risk in doing this book with me, and I am appreciative of the trust and faith he placed in me to get a manuscript to him in short order. I am, of course, also grateful to everyone who has worked behind the scenes at John Blake Publishing to get this project off the ground and to see it through to completion.

Finally, as always, I am eternally grateful to my family – Teresita, Kirsten, and Sarah – for their continued support during the often gruelling hours working on projects such as this that take me away from them. You guys are the greatest!

Author's note

The story that you are about to read is a complicated one in which the guilt or innocence of those accused is not always clear. I have made every effort to preserve the dignity of the deceased and hope that I have, at least to some extent, preserved the essence of who Meredith Kercher was in life. While the details of the murder may be repugnant to some readers, it was never my intention to offend or to appear gratuitous with regard to the homicidal violence and allegations of sexual abuse committed against this truly innocent victim.

I have been following this case closely since it first broke in November 2007, and the depiction of events herein is based on hundreds of hours of research and preparation before sitting down and writing the first word. For purposes of clarity I decided early on to present the story in chronological order, as the events unfolded, from the moments before Meredith's body was discovered, through the often confusing and complex police investigation, and to the subsequent trials and verdicts.

No attempt has been made to fictionalize any aspect of this tragic story, so none of the characters portrayed are invented or are composites from my imagination. I have attempted to present the facts of the case as they are known and as they have been presented to the public in various media formats, including newspapers, magazines, tabloids, television and radio news, and entertainment programs, as well as what happened in the courtroom at the various stages that this case has gone through. Dialogue of some of those involved was quoted from news sources that include, but is not limited to, *CNN*, *MSNBC*, *Court TV*, *Daily Mail*, *The Guardian*, *The Sunday Times*, *Corriere Della Sera*, *Corriere Dell'Umbria*, and *CBS News*, among other news outlets, as well as selected official documents that were leaked during the investigation.

While many people have come out in support of Amanda Knox, almost from the case's outset, I have refrained from doing so here because it was my intention that this book focus on what happened to Meredith and not on the media buzz surrounding Amanda. Although including some of those details has been unavoidable, I thought it best to leave those issues, for the most part, for others who will undoubtedly choose to write a book or books about the perceived 'travesty of justice' that some believe occurred in this case. I have instead attempted to maintain a neutral position with regard to the accused although, due to the complexity of the case and the media swarm that has surrounded it, this has not been easy. It was my desire to show what happened, and then let the reader decide who was truly guilty – or not – and whether or not justice has been served.

G.C.K.
DECEMBER 2009

CHAPTER 1

The medieval hillside city of Perugia, capital of the Umbrian region of Italy, situated near the Tiber River between Rome and Florence, is a notable artistic centre whose neighbouring town, Citta della Pieve, was home to painter Pietro Vannucci (also known as Perugino), who taught the great Renaissance artist Raphael. With a modern population of more than 160,000, Perugia was originally a mere settlement which historians have dated back to 310 BC. Known for having a transitional and prevalently Mediterranean climate, winters are not particularly cold and summers are pleasant and often breezy. Despite its historic past, today Perugia is renowned for its chocolate, being home to the Perugina chocolate company which makes Baci, or chocolate kisses, that are popular throughout Italy and elsewhere. The city also hosts a chocolate festival that begins in October and runs into November, enjoyed by the local residents and tourists alike.

Unfortunately, Perugia is now more widely known for the gruesome and sensational, sex-related murder of Meredith Kercher, a beautiful young foreign exchange student who succumbed to a slow and agonizing death. Meredith had moved to Perugia from her home in England to finish her studies at the Universita per Stranieri – the University of Foreigners – which attracts some 8,000 students a year from all over the world to study the Italian language and culture. The sordid details of this tragic case, as well as the questionable aspects of who had committed the crime and why, kept much of the UK and Europe riveted, especially as speculation heightened in the run-up to the Italian court's verdict in late 2009. And as one of the prime suspects was an American honor student, interest in the case crossed the Atlantic and kept many in the United States equally engrossed. It also brought into focus the apparently often wild student life in Perugia, going far beyond the intended cultural and educational enrichment of their parents' expectations, with students drifting into frequent open sexual relationships, combined with drinking and drug-taking. There were clearly dark aspects beneath the surface of this otherwise idyllic university town.

Just 21 years old at the time of her death, Meredith Susanna Cara Kercher, also known as 'Mez' to her family and friends, was born in February 1986 in the

London borough of Southwark, to an Indian mother and English father. She had a natural beauty, which some attributed to the blood mix of her parents, with flowing brown hair, brown eyes and a radiant smile sufficient to melt any young man's heart, and a personality just as pleasing as her looks. Meredith was in her third year of studies at the University of Leeds, working towards a degree in European studies when she entered the European Region Action Scheme for the Mobility of University Students (ERASMUS) student exchange programme and travelled to Italy in August 2007 to complete the course of study for her degree but primarily to study the Italian language.

It was an exciting time in her life, as it is for most her age, made all the more thrilling by being away from her home in the South London suburb of Coulsdon, living and studying in a foreign country. She made friends right away, and enjoyed the pizza and kebab restaurants that are scattered about the hillside town of Perugia. Although known as quiet and studious, she also enjoyed the nightlife that was accentuated by loud bars and dancing, but stayed away from the city's growing drug scene. She had quickly found a place to stay, in a charming little hillside villa overlooking lush foliage in the valley below, which she shared with three student housemates. However, instead of it all being the time of her life, no one could have envisaged – particularly Meredith and her family – that the move to Italy would end in a tragedy of the greatest magnitude, and that she would return home to her grieving family inside a coffin.

The investigation into the murder of Meredith Kercher officially began on Friday morning, November 2, 2007, shortly after elderly Perugia resident Elisabetta Lana, who lived near the villa that Meredith had moved into a few months earlier, pottered about in her garden, as she did nearly every morning. The air smelt fresh and cool during the morning hours, and Elisabetta paused to take in the view of the valley below with its autumn foliage colours of gold and red, and the old medieval wall visible in the distance – a reminder of its history that many Perugia residents took for granted. Suddenly Elisabetta's attention was caught by the sound of a phone or some other electronic device. She followed the sound to the end of her garden where she discovered two mobile phones. One of the phones was still ringing and Elisabetta answered it, only to receive a threatening message. Thinking it strange that two phones would have been lost or discarded by someone in her garden, on *her* property, and the fact that the message received on one of the phones had been of a threatening nature, Elisabetta called the local police to report what she had found. For all she knew, she told the police, the phones could be connected to a terrorist plot and perhaps had been somehow configured to detonate a bomb.

When the police arrived, they took custody of the

phones and quickly put to rest any fears that they were connected to a terrorist plot. Within a relatively short time, they traced one of the phones to a resident of the small villa located at 7 Via della Pergolla, in the Viale Sant'Antonio area, only a short distance from Perugia's city centre, where Meredith and her flatmates lived. The Postal and Communication Police eventually determined that both phones belonged to Meredith Kercher. Perplexed and curious as to why the phones would have ended up in Elisabetta Lana's garden, they decided that they would pay a visit to the hill-top villa where Meredith lived.

When police officers arrived, everything at first seemed quiet and normal, at least from the outside. When they knocked on the door they were greeted by a young man and a young woman. The officers announced that they were there to return the two phones, and to make inquiries as to how they had ended up in Mrs Lana's garden. The woman identified herself as Amanda Marie Knox, Meredith's 20-year-old American flatmate, who was also studying at the University of Foreigners. Amanda was an attractive blue-eyed blonde language student with a penchant for wearing denim and wool hats, described as being 'somewhat of a tomboy who enjoyed hiking'. She had chosen to study in Perugia rather than Florence, for instance, the latter being a more popular destination for students, because Perugia was much less touristy. The other person identified himself as Raffaele

Sollecito, Amanda's 24-year-old boyfriend and an Italian-born resident.

Sollecito, the son of a doctor, was in Perugia completing the final coursework for a computer science degree. The two had met only a few weeks earlier at a classical music concert, and Amanda reportedly had been attracted to him because he reminded her of Daniel Radcliffe, the actor who plays Harry Potter. Both Amanda and Sollecito expressed concern that the house may have been broken into, possibly some time during the previous evening when everyone had been out. The other residents of the apartment, Filomena Romanelli and Laura Mezzetti, were in the same age group as Meredith and Amanda.

Amanda and Raffaele explained that they had spent the evening at Sollecito's place, and had attempted to reach Meredith three times by calling one of her phones, but there had been no response. They explained that they had returned to the villa primarily because Meredith had not answered her phone. They had found the front door ajar and, strangely, the door to Meredith's room was locked – from the inside. They said that when they arrived at the cottage that morning, they discovered a broken window from the outside, as well as blood in the bathroom. Amanda said that she had initially thought that perhaps one of the other female roommates was having her menstrual period, and had failed to clean up the small amount of blood in the bathroom. She said that someone had also left a bowel movement in the toilet bowl, and had not flushed it.

The broken window was in Filomena's bedroom. Amanda said that they had already reported the possible break-in to the police after Amanda had telephoned her mother in Seattle to express her concern that 'somebody might have been in my house,' and it had been her mother that had suggested they call the police after Amanda had explained the unusual circumstances. It was not until after police officers conducted a cursory examination of the residence, consisting primarily of a walk-through of the house, during which the police confirmed the presence of blood in the bathroom and discovered for themselves that Meredith's bedroom door was locked, that they decided to break it down. Nothing could have prepared any of the officers for what they saw on the other side of the door.

From across the small room, one of the officers almost immediately saw what appeared to be a naked human foot extending from beneath a duvet, a down-filled quilt or comforter of the sort typically made with a removable cover and which is sometimes used as a mattress. Amanda, who understood Italian fairly well, and was standing outside the room, thought that she understood the word 'foot' spoken in Italian by one of the officers as, horrified, they yelled excitedly to one another. Amanda would later recall that it had been at that moment that she first realized that the police had discovered a body.

Upon entering the room, the telltale acrid, almost metallic or iron-like, smell of congealed blood was apparent, just beginning to turn slightly sweet-smelling as it began the early stages of decomposition. They noted that there was no movement from the body beneath the duvet, and each officer was suddenly filled with feelings of dread at what they knew must be done next –removal of the duvet to check for signs of life, although they instinctively knew that was unlikely.

When they tentatively pulled back the duvet, trying not to disturb any evidence that might be present, they were distressed to see the body of a young woman, semi-nude. Aghast, the police officers also saw a large amount of blood that had pooled around the upper part of the body and had soaked into the duvet, and they could see what appeared to be a number of slashing and stabbing wounds to the throat. Initially, it looked like there may have been three stab injuries to her neck, but since it was clear that she was quite dead and that no lifesaving efforts would be needed, they would leave the specifics for the detectives, coroner and forensics teams to determine. There were a number of bloodstained papers near the body, and a computer was nearby. There was little doubt in anyone's mind that the body was that of Meredith Kercher.

Although the police initially on the scene had observed bloodstains on the broken window and suspected that it had been broken outwardly, from the inside, they shut down and sealed off the premises and the surrounding area, stringing red and white police tape around the perimeter of what they believed constituted the crime scene. It was possible, they speculated, that the killer or killers may have escaped through the broken window since the door had been locked from the inside. It seemed more likely, however, that the killer or killers would have simply found it easier to leave by the front door, since no one else had apparently been at home at the time of the murder, causing some to wonder whether the window had been broken during a struggle between the victim and the killer or, perhaps, that it had been staged to appear that the window had been the killer's point of exit.

Later that day the UK Foreign Office made a simple announcement to the media: 'We can confirm that a British national was found dead in her apartment. Our consular staff is in Perugia to liaise with the Italian authorities and to provide the necessary consular assistance. The circumstances of the death are under investigation by the Italian police.'

The message had been short and to the point, although had not identified the victim's name. However, Meredith's mother, Arline, had heard one of the reports and immediately became concerned because it had involved the murder of a female British student in Perugia. She called her husband, John, a freelance journalist, who also became concerned but tried to calm his wife by telling her that there are thousands of British students in Perugia. Besides, the report, he had noted, had not mentioned any names.

In the meantime the area around the villa was inundated with police and crime-scene investigators. There was clearly more to the story of what had occurred than was initially observed, and the investigators were determined to unravel the mystery. The locals, watching the police work from a distance, no longer viewed the residence as merely a small, quiet villa, and soon began calling it *casa degli orrori* – the house of horrors.

CHAPTER 2

As the investigation into the murder of Meredith Kercher was getting underway in Perugia, back in the UK, John Kercher and his ex-wife, Arline, were growing increasingly anxious to make contact with their daughter. He recalled later that he had last spoken to Meredith at about a quarter past two on the afternoon of Thursday, November 1, while conducting business at a bank in Croydon. She had called him on his mobile phone while he was at the counter, just to ask how he was doing. Since they usually spoke during the evening hours, he had thought it a bit unusual for her to call at mid-afternoon. He, nonetheless, had been very happy to hear from her, and they had chatted for about two minutes. She had told him that she did not have classes that day because it was a public holiday. He told her that he loved her, and that he would call her back later. However, she had said

11

that she would be going out that evening, so he knew it would not be until the next day that they would be able to speak again. Although he had no way of knowing it at the time, that telephone call would be the last time he spoke to Meredith.

About 5 p.m. the following day, Friday, November 2, Arline called him about the female British student who had been murdered in Perugia. Partly because of Arline's telephone call and partly because he simply wanted to speak to his daughter again, John Kercher called Meredith on her mobile phone. To his dismay he heard an automated message that her phone was turned off. Over the next hour he tried calling Meredith a dozen times or more, keeping in mind that the time in Italy was an hour later than it was in the United Kingdom. Finally, he could hear Meredith's phone ringing in his earpiece, meaning that it had been turned back on, and he had become hopeful that she was okay and that there was nothing to worry about. However, there was still no answer. He tried calling her relentlessly over the next half hour, always with the same result: no answer.

Increasingly anxious to obtain information about the murder in Perugia to, hopefully, put his and Arline's minds at ease, Kercher telephoned the foreign desk at the *Daily Mirror*, a newspaper that he had worked for as a freelancer for a number of years, and spoke to one of his contacts there. He was told that they only had sketchy information at best at that point, but he was urged to call back in an hour or so, when they may have additional details. Although it was one of the most agonizing hours of his life, Kercher did as was suggested.

When Kercher called the newspaper back an hour later, his hopes rose again – but only for the moment. He was told that the Italian police had found the murdered girl's mobile telephone, and that they had been in touch with people in London. From that information, which was still, admittedly, sketchy, he had figured that the police in Italy must have contacted the murdered girl's family as well as British authorities. However, half an hour later a woman from the *Daily Mirror* called back and told him that they now had a name, and Kercher's hopes were quickly dashed. Although the woman seemed reluctant to provide the information to him at first for obvious reasons, she finally told him that 'The name going around Italy is Meredith.'

Numb with shock and unable to believe what he had just been told, Kercher dropped his phone thinking, hoping, praying that it had been a mistake, or that if it had not been a mistake that it was not *his* Meredith. After all, they did not have a surname yet, and Meredith was a fairly common given name. Even so, something inside his gut – instinct or intuition – told him that the murdered girl in Perugia was his daughter. Shaking and fearing the worst, he asked a friend to drive him to Arline's home, where Meredith's older sister, Stephanie, 24, along with her brothers, John, 30, and Lyle, 28, were being told to gather there too, as soon as possible. On the way Kercher telephoned the Foreign Office to try to confirm what the *Daily Mirror* had told him, but they were unable to authenticate anything at that point, and instead told him that they did not have all the details yet, and that he should not jump to any conclusions.

Within an hour, everyone had assembled at the family house. Distraught over the dreadful possibility facing them, they tried as best they could to console each other as they nervously waited for the 9 p.m. television news. Shortly after the broadcast began, their worst fears were suddenly realized as Meredith's photo appeared on the screen. In stunned disbelief, they watched and listened to precisely what they had so desperately hoped they would not see or hear – their Meredith was dead, murdered in Perugia, Italy, by a person or persons as yet unknown. As they sat there, numb with the pain of finally knowing what had happened, the Kerchers hugged each other and the tears began to flow.

The next day, as news of Meredith's tragic and untimely death spread throughout the UK, a number of Meredith's friends that she had known at school in Croydon, just south of London, made plans to place flowers at the school. John Kercher and his family learned of the plans and, emotionally moved despite their personal anguish, decided to go and meet their daughter's friends at the school. Expecting to find only a half-dozen or so people, when they arrived there were more than 70 people waiting to offer their condolences and to place their flowers in memory of Meredith. A number of people had travelled from universities at various locations around the country, and Kercher and his family found the small service held in the school's gardens 'unbelievably touching'. When the service was over, Kercher knew that they had to quickly make plans to leave for Italy.

'I was clinging to the hope that it was another Meredith, or even that they had got the name wrong,' Kercher told the *Daily Mirror*. 'But I have been told she was identified by one of her flatmates. Now I will have to go out there and identify her as her father. I can't bear to think about it.'

Meanwhile, back in Italy, the Italian news agency ANSA began reporting that the body found inside the quaint villa had been identified as Meredith Kercher, and that she had reportedly been found in her bedroom with a deep cut to her throat. ANSA also reported that Meredith had been to a Halloween party on October 31, and had watched a film at the home of some friends on the evening of November 1. According to the report, she was believed to have then left at approximately 9 p.m. ANSA also reported that police investigators had already begun questioning Meredith's friends and housemates, and among the things they learned by this time was that none of her roommates had stayed at the villa on the evening of November 1. On the surface, it appeared that Meredith had been home alone after returning from watching the movie with friends.

Forensic experts spent much of Friday evening, November 2, going over the house in a search for clues that hopefully would shed some light on how Meredith had died and the circumstances that had led up to the attack. In addition to finding the massive amounts of blood inside Meredith's bedroom, as well as the bloodstains on the frame of the broken window, investigators had also found a handkerchief outside in close proximity to a railing by the road near the villa. Its significance to the case, if any, was not yet known.

Perugia's chief prosecutor, Nicola Miriano, had already told the press that murder was the 'most credible hypothesis', but he also stated that he would not rule out other possible explanations until after he had seen the results of the forensic investigation and had read the reports of the detectives. A theory of robbery or burglary had quickly been discounted because computers, items of gold, and other valuables inside the house had not been taken.

A spokeswoman for the University of Leeds confirmed that Meredith was in the third year of a four-year European studies degree programme at the time of her death. In addition to Italian language coursework, Meredith was also studying modern history, political theory and cinema history. She said that the university officials were shocked and dismayed over Meredith's death, and expressed concern for Meredith's family and friends, and added that the university was sending a member of its staff 'to provide support to her fellow students'.

On the evening of Friday November 2, a few of Meredith's friends paid tribute to their dead friend on the Internet social networking site, Facebook. One wrote: 'Meredith, words cannot express how I feel right now. I'm thinking of you and can't believe that one minute we were celebrating Halloween together, and then the next you're gone. You're in my thoughts and prayers.'

Another friend wrote: 'Love you now and always. The memories that we have made together will always stay in my heart! Xxxxx.'

A number of photographs of Meredith and her friends taken at one of the Halloween parties they had attended two nights earlier were also posted on Facebook. Some depicted Meredith dressed up as a vampire, with fake blood made to appear as if it was dripping from her mouth.

In a recent message to one of her friends, Meredith had said that she was happy and enjoying Perugia, and 'Was having a good time... it's starting to get really cold now, but the chocolate festival is on at the moment, so a good excuse to drink a lot of hot chocolate.'

Meanwhile, as they wrapped up the first day of their investigation, police said that they were looking for the murder weapon, believed to be a knife, screwdriver, or a shard of broken glass. 'This was a particularly nasty murder and the victim was found with a deep cut to her throat,' said an unidentified law enforcement source, who declined to provide any additional information at that time. But as additional details began to be released, it was revealed that Meredith had planned to return home the following Friday to attend a birthday celebration for her mother.

The ANSA news agency reported that magistrate Giuliano Mignini had been assigned to lead the investigation, and that a postmortem examination of Meredith's body was scheduled to be performed by the pathologist Luca Lalli.

CHAPTER 3

Meredith Kercher was described by family and friends as a quiet young woman, diligent and serious about her studies, who loved to read. She aspired to become a teacher after completing her education, and enjoyed writing stories and poetry. During her teens she studied ballet as well as martial arts, in particular karate. Having a great sense of humour, Meredith could make people laugh and put them at ease.

'She had such life and vitality and made friends, wherever she went,' her father said. 'The sense of the ridiculous stayed with her. Meredith really enjoyed Halloween.'

During her childhood, she often made Halloween costumes from plastic bin liners, and would go out with family members to visit neighbours, as part of the traditional celebrations, which some view as macabre.

As her father remarked, it was ironic that she died so horribly only one day after Halloween.

As Italian investigators continued piecing together Meredith's last known movements and interviewed her contacts, they learned that she and her friends, including roommate Amanda Knox, had spent at least a part of the evening of October 31, Halloween Night, at a party in the ground floor flat of the villa, the home of Giacomo Silenzi, a young Italian man Meredith had been dating. It was also believed that she may have attended other parties that night. Meredith spent the following evening with two girlfriends, Sophie Purton and Robyn Butterworth, also from the UK. They had dinner at Robyn's apartment, and then watched the movie, *The Notebook*, on DVD. Meredith, tired from the partying that she had enjoyed the previous evening, decided to call it an early night and left Robyn's apartment shortly before 9 p.m.

Sophie walked her part of the way home, and the two girls said goodnight to each other on a street corner not far from the cottage where Meredith lived. Investigators believe that Meredith probably arrived home around 9.15 p.m., and initially theorized that she had been killed sometime between then and midnight. The police officer leading the investigation, Marco Chiacchiera, head of the investigative unit known as the Perugia Flying Squad, which was being assisted by forensic teams from Rome, soon revised the estimated time of the murder to sometime between 10 p.m. Thursday and 10 a.m. Friday.

Although more than 100 police officers had been brought to Perugia from all across Italy to assist in the investigation, by Saturday, November 3, the police still had not named any suspects. But revealing additional bits of information, Chiacchiera said that Meredith had been found wearing only a T-shirt, and that her throat had been cut by a knife or other sharp object that had been thrust in an upward motion with much force. There were signs of other injuries, but Chiacchiera did not go into the details at that time.

'We have 100 officers on this case and are not ruling out any possibilities,' Chiacchiera said. 'We are now questioning all of Kercher's friends, male and female.'

Chiacchiera added that there was no evidence of a sexual attack, although it would later be revealed that there was evidence of the possibility of recent consensual sexual intercourse. He said that it was possible that the killer may have entered Meredith's bedroom via a window –despite it being 13 feet from the ground – and exited by the front door after stopping in the bathroom to wash off blood, a possible explanation for the traces of blood that had been found there. Chiacchiera indicated that it was likely that Meredith had known her killer, because there was no evidence that the villa's front door, which had been left unlocked, had been forced. Although Meredith's body had been found locked inside her bedroom, investigators had so far not found the key to the door, leaving unanswered the important question of whether her killer had entered or exited – or both – through the broken window in her room.

It was not long before speculation began to surface that Meredith may have been attacked by a boyfriend. However, the conjecture was quickly dismissed by her friends and acquaintances, including a pub owner she knew, who said that although she was known to go on dates at times she had not been, to the best of their knowledge, in a relationship at the time of her death.

Chiacchiera soon learned that Meredith and Amanda Knox had met when each had responded to a notice appealing for roommates that they had seen at the university. Although they were opposites in many ways, with Meredith being quiet and reserved and Amanda being more lively and boisterous, the couple of Italians who shared the villa told the police that the two girls had initially hit it off and had seemed to like each other. Among the things they seemed to have in common were that both were humanities students, both enjoyed drinking in Perugia's lively pub scene, both played guitar, and both girls liked to smoke pot. However, as time went on, Meredith and Amanda drifted apart. Meredith did not like the fact that Amanda had so many frequent visitors, many of whom were male, and she did not like Amanda's sense of hygiene and was particularly bothered by the fact that Amanda frequently did not flush the toilet after using it. Nonetheless, they made the best of their situation despite their obvious differences.

Forensic experts worked through the weekend at the murder scene, collecting and analyzing fingerprints and collecting items where DNA might be present. A footprint made in blood was also found near Meredith's body, and the chemical Luminol (which highlights traces of blood) was used throughout the dwelling to help investigators identify other locations where blood evidence might be present. They also reportedly found fingerprints on Meredith's two mobile phones, and the call records were being examined.

Chiacchiera and his investigators expanded their avenue of inquiry to include the Halloween photos, and others, that had been posted on Facebook, in an effort to identify people in the pictures with Meredith. Some of the photos were taken at pubs in Perugia, including the Merlin Pub, co-owned by Pasquale Alessi, where Meredith liked to hang out. A number of the photos had been taken at the Merlin during a party there on Halloween night. Alessi helped the investigators identify people in the photos with Meredith, including a part-time bouncer at one of Perugia's pubs, a male American student, and a Libyan computer student. Gennaro Crugliano, 33, who took some of the photographs, also helped police confirm some of the identities.

By that time speculation about how Meredith was murdered, who murdered her, why she was murdered, and so forth, was running rampant in Perugia. One rumour suggested that she had been murdered by a man that she had met at one of the parties she had attended on Halloween.

'She was not the type to invite someone home without knowing them very well,' Crugliano said in an effort to dispel the gossip.

'I was with Meredith at the pub that night and did not see her meet anyone,' said another of her friends, Samantha Rodenhurst, 20, also a classmate of Meredith's at the university. 'Meredith had not received any threats as far as I know.'

Other people came forward to help dismiss much of the gossip that was being disseminated throughout Perugia, but it did not seem to help matters much. This was a huge story for Perugia, and it ranked as one of the biggest in all of Italy, perhaps even overshadowing the 'Monster of Florence' case (the still unsolved murders that took place in Florence between 1968 and 1985). The rumours, as everyone would see, were not going to go away easily.

On Sunday, November 4, the same day that the autopsy on Meredith's body had been scheduled, an unusual, even ghoulish event occurred at the entrance to the University of Foreigners. Someone had posted a notice advertising for an English student to rent a vacant room at the villa where Meredith had lived. Whoever posted the notice included a bogus telephone number that comprised of the date of Meredith's murder. It was removed by the police as soon as it came to their attention, but they did not trace who had posted it.

Later that evening the pathologist Luca Lalli performed the postmortem examination of Meredith's body. Afterwards, Lalli said that the autopsy had shown that Meredith 'possibly' had sexual relations prior to her death, but that she 'was not raped'. His findings helped refute some of the false information – including that she had been raped – that was beginning to creep into the Italian press. Lalli also said that he believed the weapon that was used to kill Meredith had been a penknife.

Following the autopsy, the Italian press reported that Meredith's carotid artery had not been cut, resulting in the theory that she had probably endured a relatively slow and agonizing death as she bled, choking on her own blood. As additional details of the postmortem on Meredith's corpse were either reported directly or leaked – as many of the details would be – information surfaced indicating that she was also strangled, that her throat had been crushed, and that her partially-nude body had sustained 47 cuts and bruises. There was also talk that the police now believed that Meredith had died while attempting to fend off a sexual attack and that police now believed that the broken bedroom window had been staged. Adding to the growing mystery was a report that Amanda Knox had been seen at a launderette on Via

Fabretti on the morning of November 2, in the company of a black man from North Africa, washing clothes and a pair of shoes, leaving many people wondering where all the twists and turns would eventually lead.

What seemed particularly troubling to the police and Mignini early on were the wounds on Meredith's body, details of which were initially kept from the press. It was eventually revealed that Meredith had sustained three large knife wounds that most likely resulted in her death, but she had also been subjected to a series of 'pinprick' knife wounds, which could suggest torture or, perhaps, some kind of sadistic sexual game that had been perpetrated by her attacker or attackers, a game that had eventually spun out of control because of the unwillingness of the victim to participate.

CHAPTER 4

In any investigation of great intensity, and this case certainly fitted that bill, the police typically interview persons of interest, witnesses and suspects, multiple times, in part to flesh out additional details just in case something had been missed or overlooked earlier, and in part to find discrepancies in the answers of those being questioned. The Meredith Kercher investigation was no different, except, perhaps, with regard to the increased intensity of the questioning, and the fact that the so-called discrepancies that surfaced during the interrogations would eventually centre on the changing of stories regarding what had occurred in the hours preceding Meredith's death.

Amanda Knox typically kept in touch with her mother, Edda Mellas, 46, back home in Seattle, via e-mail. However, with a nine-hour time difference between Perugia and Seattle, Amanda had instead telephoned her mother on November 2, waking her up during the early morning hours to tell her how she had returned to her apartment to take a shower after spending the night at Raffaele Sollecito's apartment, only to find things amiss at her own place. For example, she had told her mother that she had noticed that the door to the flat had been open, and, once inside, she had noticed some of the issues in the bathroom – someone had left a bowel movement in the toilet, for instance. It had not been a long telephone call because Amanda had told her mother that she was returning to Sollecito's apartment straight away. What seemed unusual about this account of the events was that it had made it appear, if one could believe the media reports, that Amanda had first returned to the villa alone to take a shower, before going back to Sollecito's apartment, only to retrace her steps to the villa – with Sollecito – a short time later. Amanda would also later tell the police officers that she had noticed the spots or drops of blood in the bathroom.

Apparently, Amanda had also called one of her roommates, Filomena Romanelli, that morning, and had repeated much of what she had told her mother – that the front door had been open, and that there were bloodstains on the bathroom floor. She had also purportedly told Filomena that she was returning to her boyfriend's apartment to bring him back to the villa, but that she was going to take a shower first.

When the police had arrived at the villa to return Meredith's mobile telephones, Amanda had said in her first statements that she had received a text message from Patrick Lumumba, owner of the Le Chic pub where she worked, telling her that she did not have to report for work that evening. Le Chic was popular with students and other young people, and Amanda worked part-time waiting at tables. She had responded by writing, 'See you later. Have a good evening!' As a result of not having to go in to work, she said that she and Sollecito had spent the evening of November 1 together at his flat, smoking pot and watching the French film, *Amelie*, starring Audrey Tatou. They had also made love, and had eaten a late dinner. She also said that she had read part of a Harry Potter book at Sollecito's flat. However, the investigators had seen the book at the villa, not at Sollecito's, and noted that she had not said anything about bringing it there from Sollecito's. Sollecito, meanwhile, had told the police that he had worked at his computer most of the evening, and said that when he and Amanda had returned to the villa shortly before the police arrived with Meredith's telephones, that he had been attempting to call the police to report what he believed had been a break-in at the villa after noticing the shattered window. Up to that point, with a few exceptions, Amanda's and Sollecito's accounts of the events appeared to corroborate each other's whereabouts on the night Meredith was killed.

However, over the next few days – between Friday, November 2 and the following Tuesday – the police would bring in Amanda and Raffaele for questioning a number of times, and they would also examine Raffaele's computer and begin looking at each of their mobile phone records with a fine-tooth comb, after which the inconsistencies began to mount.

Recalling that Raffaele had said that he had used his computer most of the evening of November 1, the investigators naturally examined it in an effort to validate his statement. However, they found that it had not, in fact, been used most of the evening as Raffaele had stated. Investigators also noted that both Amanda's and Raffaele's mobile phones had been turned off sometime between 8.00 and 8.30 p.m. on November 1, and had remained turned off until the next morning, which was not consistent with their normal phone usage routines.

Raffaele's phone records showed another inconsistency. When the police had arrived at the villa to return Meredith's phones, Raffaele had told them that he had been trying to call the police to report what he considered a break-in; however, the records showed that he had begun making those calls to the police *after* the officers arrived to return Meredith's phones. Both Amanda and Raffaele had also insisted in their initial statements to the police that they had no idea that Meredith lay dead inside her locked bedroom.

Interestingly, it was not long before investigators

produced a witness, Marco Quintavalle, who operated a small shop. Quintavalle told them that a young woman, who he identified as Amanda Knox, had come into his shop early on the morning of November 2, during the time-frame in which she had claimed to have been at Raffaele's flat. Police noted that Raffaele's apartment had smelt of bleach that morning, and they had reportedly found a receipt from Quintavalle's shop at his flat. Although the police did not say if the receipt showed what had been purchased at Quintavalle's shop that morning, the implication was that they believed bleach and possibly other cleaning supplies had been purchased there and may have been used by Raffaele and Amanda to clean themselves up, and possibly to clean a murder weapon.

Now that the villa had been completely sealed off and designated as a crime scene, Amanda Knox, along with her two Italian roommates, was essentially homeless, at least in Perugia. By Sunday, November 4, Amanda's mother was already en route to Italy from her home in Seattle so that she could be with her daughter, who had said that she wanted to remain in Perugia to finish her term at the university and to assist the police in their investigations. Believing that she was travelling to Italy to help her daughter find a new place in which to reside, Edda Mellas would be in for a shock upon her late-night arrival in Perugia when she would learn that Amanda was, by then, being regarded as a possible suspect in Meredith's murder. She would later tell a reporter for *Radar* magazine that the news about her daughter's predicament had made her physically ill. She spent her first morning there searching for an attorney to represent Amanda but, of course, had no idea of just how bad things would become over the coming hours, days, weeks and months.

In the meantime, as police activity was gearing up in Perugia, Meredith's family back home in England released a statement on Monday, November 5, through London's Metropolitan Police. It read in part: 'Words cannot even begin to describe how we feel right now, other than utterly devastated at the tragic loss of our daughter and sister, Meredith. Nothing can prepare you for the news we received on Friday evening and it has taken this long for us to feel able to express our thoughts.

'Mez was someone very special – a 21-year-old who was into her studies, worked hard and enjoyed spending time socializing with her friends and family. She was one of the most beautiful, intelligent, witty and caring people you could wish to meet. Nothing was ever too much effort for her – a loving daughter and sister and a loyal friend.

'Meredith went to Italy at the end of August as part of her undergraduate degree course and was excited at the prospect of spending the year there to improve her language skills, make new friends and immerse herself in the culture. She was pursuing her dream and we can take some comfort in knowing that she has left us at what was a very happy time in her life. We feel it is no exaggeration to say that Meredith touched the lives of everyone she met with her infectious, upbeat personality, smile and sense of humour.'

In closing their statement, the family said: 'We appeal to anyone who may have any information, no matter how trivial it may seem, to contact their police and help us bring to justice the person who destroyed so many lives.'

When the Italian media, and later news outlets all over Europe, began reporting that Meredith had been lured into a sexual rendezvous with one or more of those responsible for her death – allegations made in part because of the partially nude manner in which her body had been found and because of speculation voiced to the press by certain members of the police – Meredith's father, naturally, as any father would, downplayed the reports, stating publicly that Meredith would never have been involved in such things. Her character was viewed by those who knew her as a wholesome young woman and not someone who could have been drawn into any kind of sexual tryst. She had clearly been victimized, and her death had been caused by the violent actions of 'an unidentified person or persons', according to Nicola Miriano, the magistrate involved with her case. The cuts and bruises found on her body as reported by the pathologist who conducted the autopsy, Luca Lalli, also served to bolster the theory that whatever had occurred to Meredith that night, she had been an unwilling participant who had died while fighting off what appeared to have been a sexual attack. Lalli had determined that there was evidence of sexual activity prior to her death, but he stopped short of saying that she had been raped.

As the investigation went on, homicide detectives continued in their efforts to identify and question Meredith's known friends and acquaintances in Perugia. Investigators also examined her diary and her laptop computer in their search for evidence and, according to press reports, were looking at an employee of a local bar as a potential suspect. Detectives also continued to scrutinize the route that Meredith had taken home alone, through Piazza Grimana, the night she was killed. A basketball court in the piazza was a known hangout for drug addicts at night, and they had to consider the possibility that perhaps one or more of the addicts had followed her home that evening. Although closed circuit television (CCTV) cameras can be found throughout Perugia, there are none in the piazza, making the location a favourite haunt for addicts and other undesirable types – particularly at night.

One aspect of the piazza that initially caught some attention was the fact that a known drug dealer, himself an addict, had been seen a few hours prior to the discovery of Meredith's body, covered with blood and bearing a large cut to one of his hands. He was reportedly seen washing himself off in a public water fountain where he was heard screaming on a telephone, '*I killed her. I killed her.*' Although a television reporter had successfully substantiated the reports about the addict, and had found a number of witnesses – including an ambulance driver and an emergency medical technician who had been dispatched to the piazza to treat the man's injury and whisk him off to a hospital – the incident was ultimately dismissed by the police and prosecutor Mignini.

Mignini went to great lengths to get the reporter to back away from her story, largely by charging her with attempting to inflame fear and panic throughout the community by writing and publishing bogus information. Mignini's team and the police, it seemed, had ascertained that the young man had been screaming at his girlfriend over the telephone, but they failed to adequately explain why he had thought that he had killed a woman, or even *who* he thought he had killed. Although the paramedics had removed him from the piazza and had taken him to a hospital, he was later transferred to a facility for drug addicts where he was kept under near-constant observation.

It appeared that Mignini and the police were far more intrigued with Amanda Knox and Raffaele Sollecito, especially after learning that Sollecito, a wealthy doctor's son from the southern Italian city of Bari, on the Adriatic coast, allegedly liked to carry knives on his person, and perhaps because investigators had found a number of violent comic books, such as Japanese *manga* comics, as well as other violent reading material, in Raffaele's apartment. Some of the comics had featured illustrated stories about killing female vampires on Halloween night, prompting recollections of how Meredith had dressed up as a vampire for Halloween and had attended a number of parties prior to her murder and how, police would later contend, some of the comics' illustrations and descriptions were in some ways similar to the murder scene in Meredith's bedroom.

As the weekend came to a close, as Mignini and the police continued to look for ways to solve and build their case, local residents who had known Meredith planned a candlelight vigil outside Perugia cathedral, and had draped a banner bearing her name from the nearby town hall. Several people handed out flyers announcing the vigil, which read: 'With greatest love from all your friends in Perugia. Addio, Meredith.'

The fact that Meredith was so well-loved by people in a country so far from her own only served to add to the mystique surrounding why anyone would want to kill her with such unleashed savagery. It just did not make any sense.

CHAPTER 5

Although many of the participants in the case did not know it yet, by the afternoon of Monday November 5, 2007, the Meredith Kercher murder case was on the verge of taking a dramatic turn. Amanda Knox, dressed in the typical vintage-style clothing that she liked so much, along with her boyfriend, Raffaele Sollecito, were hauled into a Perugia police station for what the two starry-eyed lovers thought would be simply another round of routine questioning. This time, however, was different. They were each placed in separate rooms, and the questioning lasted throughout the night. Amanda's mother, Edda Mellas, had been in the Italian city for only a few hours and as the evening wore on she was increasingly aghast at what was happening to her daughter. In the midst of an aura of disbelief, she had not yet found a lawyer for Amanda and probably would not be able to do so until the following day.

Since they had been placed in separate interrogation rooms, Amanda and Raffaele could neither see nor hear each other during the questioning by police, who were speaking in Italian and utilizing typical interrogation techniques used by police around the globe – the interrogators told Amanda that Raffaele had placed her at the crime scene, and vice versa. Although the pair had initially told investigators the same story regarding their activities and whereabouts the night Meredith was killed, at various points during the long night of questioning the police would convince them that each had turned against the other. In fact, before the night was over, Amanda and Raffaele would each change their stories, and the new accounts that they provided would be markedly different from what they had said at the outset of the investigation.

The interrogation rooms at the police station were dingy, cold and dismal, with a smell of stale cigarette smoke. The lighting felt intimidating, made all the more so by the uncomfortable institutional chairs and the pacing back and forth of the tireless inquisitors. It was intended to be that way, an aid to help the interrogators wear down the suspects.

The police learned a lot during the questioning which lasted over the Monday evening and into early Tuesday morning. Although the investigators had brought the pair in for questioning several times over the previous couple of days, the interrogation that began on Monday afternoon had been the longest and most intensive and, many would later say, the most telling. By the time it was over, a number of those who had been critical of the tactics being employed by Mignini and the police began to wonder whether the controversial prosecutor may have been on the right track after all in going after Amanda and Raffaele to the exclusion of other potential suspects. In fairness to the police and the prosecutor there were many details, of course, that had not yet been made public and would later weigh heavily in their decisions regarding how they handled the case.

Convinced by his interrogators that Amanda had placed him at the scene of Meredith's murder, Raffaele at one point told the police that it was possible that Amanda could have left his apartment, perhaps around 9.00 p.m., killed Meredith in her bedroom, and returned afterwards to his apartment and pretended that all was well and that nothing out of the ordinary had occurred that evening. He thought that she had been gone for about four hours, but his statement seemed less than convincing. After all, he had said that his memory was clouded from smoking marijuana and hashish with Amanda, and it was difficult for him to remember precise details about the evening. However, here is part of what he purportedly told the police during questioning:

'I don't remember how she was dressed, or if she was dressed differently from before when we said goodbye. I don't remember if we had sex that evening.'

This seemed to contradict his original story that he and Amanda had watched *Amelie*, ate dinner, and made love the night Meredith died.

'The next morning, we woke around ten and she told me she wanted to go home to have a shower and change her clothes,' he continued. 'She told me that when she got home she had found the door open and traces of blood in the small bathroom. She asked me if it seemed strange. I said to her it was.'

Raffaele said that when he returned to the villa with Amanda, the room of another housemate had been in disarray, while he noticed that Amanda's room had been neat and tidy.

'Then I went to Meredith's door and saw it was locked,' he said. 'First, I checked to see if it was true what Amanda had said about the blood in the bathroom, and I noticed drops of blood in the basin. On the mat there was something strange, a sort of mixture of water and blood, while the rest of the bathroom was clean and tidy. Amanda came into the bathroom and she hugged me tight. I tried to force the door, but couldn't, and at that point I decided to call my sister for advice because she is a Carabinieri officer. She told me to dial 112 [the Italian emergency number] but at that moment the police arrived.'

Raffaele reportedly indicated that his previous

statement to the police had been a 'load of bollocks because she had convinced me of her version of the facts and I didn't think anything different.'

Similarly, when confronted with portions of Raffaele's statement, Amanda had told the investigators that it was possible that Raffaele had awakened during the night, slipped out of his flat and murdered Meredith, only to return to his own bed where Amanda presumably was fast asleep.

As the questioning continued and investigators asked her about other possible scenarios that may have occurred the night Meredith was murdered, Amanda, by now growing tired and weary, said that she could have been at the villa that night and may have heard someone screaming. It was during this so-called admission that the case took a very different turn – Amanda implicated her Congolese boss at Le Chic, Patrick Diya Lumumba, 38, by saying that she and Lumumba could have gone to the villa that evening together. The police, aware of the text messaging that had occurred between Amanda and Lumumba on the night of Meredith's murder, had been pressing her for additional information about the bar owner, in part because the hair from a black man had been found in one of Meredith's hands – a fact that previously had been kept from the public.

'I don't remember if my friend Meredith was already there or whether she came later,' Amanda said during questioning. 'We were all separate. What I can say is that the two of them [Lumumba and Meredith] went off together... into Meredith's room while I think I stayed in the kitchen... he wanted her... yes, we were in the house... that evening we wanted to have a bit of fun. We were drunk. We asked her to join us. Diya [Patrick] wanted her. Raffaele and I went into another room, and then I heard screams. Patrick and Meredith were in Meredith's bedroom while I think I stayed in the kitchen. I can't remember how long they were in the bedroom together – I can only say that at a certain point I heard Meredith screaming and I was so frightened I put my fingers in my ears... In my mind, I saw Patrick in confused images... I don't remember anything after that. My head is really confused... there is such a lot going on in my head... I don't remember if Meredith called out or if I heard thuds because I was upset, but I can imagine what was happening... I want to tell you what has happened because it's left me really shocked and I am really scared of Patrick, the African guy who owns Le Chic where I sometimes work... I'm not sure whether Raffaele was there too that evening, but I do remember waking up at his house in his bed and that in the morning I went back to where I lived, where I found the door open.'

The investigators could not help but wonder why Amanda had changed her story regarding Raffaele. First she had said that he had been at the house with her, Patrick and Meredith, but a little later on she had contradicted her earlier statement. Was she truly confused about the events of that evening? Or had she contradicted herself to further confuse the situation?

Portions of the statement found their way into a number of newspapers in Italy including *Corriere Della Sera*. The news, of course, travelled quickly, and the details of what Amanda purportedly told the police also appeared in newspapers in the UK, the European continent, as well as the United States.

According to a police interpreter, Anna Donnino, Amanda had seemed somewhat relieved after she had changed her story to the admission that she had been at home and had heard Meredith's screams. Amanda had also reportedly told the police that Lumumba had been infatuated with Meredith, but the reality of what may or may not have been said was not immediately known, because the police refused to release any of the tapes recorded during the interrogations.

What *was* known at this juncture was that Lumumba had first met Meredith at Le Chic in October, when she had told him that she knew how to make *mojitos*, a Cuban cocktail that normally consists of lime juice, sugar cane sticks, mint and rum, after seeing that he stocked Polish vodka in the bar. He had purportedly invited Meredith to return at some point to make the vodka variation of the drink.

Amanda had also told police interrogators that she had met Lumumba at a basketball court on the evening of Meredith's murder, and that they had arrived at her villa at approximately 9.00 p.m.

Lumumba, however, would later insist that he had spent the evening at his bar.

At dawn on Monday, November 6, with Mignini and Perugia's chief of police, Arturo De Felice, believing that they now had sufficient evidence, arrested Amanda and Raffaele and made a grandstand appearance before the press to announce the arrests. Naturally, the story quickly became the biggest news item to hit Perugia in years, and it did not take long for news broadcasts to proliferate around the world. The police chief named Amanda as the ringleader of the brutal crime, and said that Meredith's murder 'was probably a sexually motivated killing.'

De Felice was quick to add that the trio – Amanda, Raffaele and Patrick Lumumba – had killed Meredith because she had refused to participate in an orgy that had involved the use of drugs. He praised the work of his detectives as 'magnificent', and said that the case was now closed after barely five days' worth of work in which investigators had 'worked around the clock' to solve it because 'the city needed a result quickly'.

'It's an ugly story in which people which this girl had in her home – friends – tried to force her into relations which she didn't want,' Italian Foreign Minister Giuliano Amato told the news conference.

Whether Amanda had seen the line of questioning about Lumumba as an opportunity to shift suspicion away from her and Raffaele, or whether the events that she had described were true, was not immediately known. The case was under judicial seal, at least officially, though it was obvious that the information that was making its way into the press was being leaked. The detectives had a summary of Amanda's statement typed up and asked that she sign it, although it would later be ruled inadmissible because she did not have a lawyer present to represent her and also because the questioning had occurred in Italian. Nonetheless, it was deemed sufficient cause for investigators to arrest Lumumba and bring him in for questioning, which they did early on Wednesday, November 7. Before Lumumba's arrest, however, some time on the evening of November 6, Amanda changed her story again and recanted her confession in a statement she wrote to the police.

'In regards to this "confession" that I made last night,' Amanda wrote in her statement, 'I want to make clear that I'm very doubtful of the verity of my statements because they were made under the pressures of stress, shock, and extreme exhaustion... These things seem unreal to me, like in a dream, and I am unsure if they are real things that happened to me or are just dreams my head has made to try to answer the questions...'

Amanda returned to the original version of the events that she had related to police during her first interviews, and stated that during the later, all-night interrogation she had been confused because investigators had asked her to imagine certain scenarios, such as other people who may have been interested in Meredith. She also alleged that she had been struck by the police during the latest round of questioning, which would serve to introduce charges of police brutality. As far as her accusations against Lumumba were concerned, the police interrogators had appeared angry and Amanda had struggled to find answers to their queries. It had been the police, after all, who had brought up the line of questioning regarding Lumumba as they focused on the text messaging that had occurred between him and Amanda the night Meredith was killed.

It was later learned that Lumumba, described by the locals as 'very educated' and as a 'gentle' person who was 'willing to help anybody', had been one of the people passing out flyers announcing the candlelight vigil in honour of Meredith's memory. He had also done a lot of volunteer work at the University for Foreigners, and was known for being very generous with his time, even when it meant reduced hours for his own recreation. It transpired that he was well-known in Perugia, in large part because of his bar, which he had opened in August 2007 (the same month that Meredith had arrived in town). Born in the Democratic Republic of Congo in 1969, and believed to be related to the Congolese Prime Minister, Patrice Lumumba (who was assassinated in 1961) he immigrated to Italy in 1988. The student community also knew him because of his involvement in helping organize concerts and other musical experiences – he frequently performed in his own band, which had a repertoire of reggae and contemporary music.

Lumumba, who wore his hair in short, tight dreadlocks, was in a loving relationship with a young Polish woman, named Ola, whom he had met while she was studying Italian at the University for Foreigners, where Lumumba had also studied nearly twenty years earlier. After deciding that she would remain in Italy, Ola worked as a waitress in a busy restaurant and the couple moved into an apartment together. They had a child, who was barely a year old at the time of Lumumba's arrest.

Lumumba was comfortable wearing jeans, pullover shirts, and zippered jackets as part of his everyday attire, and people said that he typically had a kind smile on his face. The smile, however, was missing the morning he was arrested and handcuffed by police officers, and was replaced with an incredulous expression that depicted confusion, anger, and above all, disbelief about the predicament that he now found himself in.

One of Lumumba's neighbours, according to the *Corriere dell'Umbria*, reportedly heard Lumumba shouting, 'I haven't done anything,' as he was being handcuffed and placed inside a police car.

As news of Lumumba's arrest as a murder suspect spread through the city, shock and disbelief was also on the minds of many of the students, as well as others who knew him, including Esteban Garcia Pascual, owner of the popular student hangout, La Tana Dell'Orso, where Lumumba had worked occasionally as a DJ prior to opening Le Chic.

'This is like a hammer blow to the head,' Pascual said after hearing of Lumumba's arrest. 'I've known him since 1999, and I can't believe it... he is very friendly and professional.' Pascual said that Lumumba was a gentle and relaxed person. 'He worked at the university organizing cultural events and concerts, and is from a really respectable family. He is a nice person... very friendly and professional.'

Prior to his arrest, Lumumba was seen mingling with students, journalists and friends of Meredith outside the university. He purportedly told one reporter that he liked Meredith, and had been planning to give her a job handing out advertising leaflets for Le Chic.

When it became clear that the police believed they had built a solid case against their three suspects, the pathologist, Luca Lalli, who had performed the autopsy on Meredith's body, made another statement to the press that was related to his earlier comments in which he had suggested that Meredith had sex before she was killed, but still refrained from calling it rape.

'The autopsy showed no sign of the lesions that suggest rape, but I cannot rule out intercourse under threat, which might not have the same signs,' Lalli said. 'I feel free to say that, now that the police have a break in the investigation.'

If Meredith had been forced, or coerced, into having sexual relations under threat or duress, would that not be the same as rape? Many people reading the various accounts of the case now wondered about the legal definition of rape, but considering that there was nothing of evidentiary value that conclusively showed that Meredith had been raped had little choice but to accept the Italian authorities' theory about what had happened that night. People also believed the assertion made by the police that Meredith knew her assailants, because of the lack of forced entry to the house.

Meanwhile, Meredith's parents, along with her sister, who had been in Perugia to identify Meredith's body and to be brought up to date with what was happening regarding the investigation, had to leave to return to London on Wednesday, November 7. Prior to leaving, however, John Kercher, in a very poignant gesture on the family's behalf, left a note on the steps of Perugia's cathedral, facing the city's square, which read: 'Love you forever, Meredith. All my love, Dad. Xxxx.'

CHAPTER 6

It was not long before the nickname 'Foxy Knoxy' – one that came from her skills on the football pitch – was taken from Amanda Knox's own MySpace page, and appeared in media reports of Amanda's involvement in the Meredith Kercher murder case. And within a day or two of her arrest, images from the social networking MySpace page also began appearing all over the Internet, depicting her as a heartless villain with a voracious sexual appetite. But it did not end merely with portraying Amanda as a 'man-eater'. It seemed that within hours of the dissemination of news about her MySpace site, a story, also found on her page, about two brothers conversing about the drugging and rape of a female, began finding its way around the Internet. Not helping matters for Amanda – who was being described as a wholesome, warm and adventurous person by her acquaintances, friends, and relatives – was the way the Italian press and British tabloids jumped on the bandwagon that was rolling out a portrayal of her as the 'Dark Lady of Seattle' or 'La luciferina', loosely translated as an angel-faced devil. To top it all off, such a disparaging portrayal of the young woman with icy blue eyes – whether true or false – was only just beginning.

Born on July 9, 1987, in Seattle, Washington, Amanda Knox grew up in the typically quiet west side working-class area that is situated along picturesque Puget Sound. Characterized as a bright student in high school, Amanda won a partial scholarship to the Seattle Preparatory School, an esteemed and prestigious private school that was affiliated with Seattle University. The school was a long commute from her home, but she made the trip five days a week with excellent attendance, only rarely missing a day. Although homework assignments were often extensive, she always seemed to find the time to participate in soccer, one of her favourite sports, and drama. She also enjoyed rock climbing, and some would say later that the sport had given her much strength in her hands and fingers – the type of strength needed, for instance, to hold someone down during a violent struggle.

Following graduation from high school, Amanda was readily accepted at the University of Washington, also in Seattle, where she studied German, Japanese, Italian and creative writing. It was later said that the 'dark' short story about the drugging and rape of a young woman that she had placed on her MySpace page had been written in one of her university creative writing classes. The story involved two brothers, Kyle and Edgar, and Kyle says at one point: 'A thing you have to know about chicks is that they don't know what they want.' *Kyle winked his eye.* 'You have to show it to them. Trust me.' *He cocked his eyebrows up and one side of his mouth rose into a grin.* 'I think we both know hard A is hardly a drug.'

When she had the opportunity to study in Italy for a year, Amanda jumped at it. She left for Europe in late summer 2007 and arrived in Italy in August via a trip through Germany, where she visited relatives. Once in Perugia she settled into the villa with the three other girls, started her college courses, and found the part-time job at Le Chic.

Many people close to Amanda, and who were supporting her through the ordeal involving Meredith's murder, said that she was a kind and caring girl and that the type of crime she had been charged with was totally out of character, and that she was not capable of murder. However, the picture being portrayed of her by investigators, the judiciary, and the media in Italy was markedly different.

For example, while friends and acquaintances of Meredith, many of whom also knew Amanda and Raffaele, had been visibly upset during questioning by police, Amanda and Raffaele behaved affectionately toward one another during police questioning, which seemed unusual considering the circumstances. And according to Monica Napoleoni, head of homicide in Perugia, Amanda had remained quiet and calm during questioning, while at one point had been seen doing cartwheels and splits at the police station. However, when taken in for fingerprinting, according to D'Astolto, she had paced back and forth and had hit herself on the head – possibly in the realisation of the significant role that such evidence might play in her future.

Another occurrence that did not serve to help Amanda's case early on was when police interpreter Aida Colontane, and a roommate from the villa, reported seeing a red welt on Amanda's neck, that some would speculate could have been caused during a struggle with Meredith. Police would also report that despite earlier suggestions that Amanda's fingerprints had been found inside Meredith's bedroom, only one fingerprint belonging to Amanda had been found inside the cottage – strange considering she lived there. This led the police to deduce that the cottage had been cleaned after Meredith's death. The police also said that a hand impression possibly made by Amanda had been found on Meredith's head. As information continued to be revealed slowly, forensic investigators would report that they had identified fresh blood – both Meredith's and Amanda's – in the bathroom sink that they shared.

It seemed evident that even early on in the investigation, nearly everyone – with the exception of Amanda's friends, relatives and staunchest supporters – including the police and the press in the UK and Italy, suspected Amanda might be responsible for Meredith's murder. Newspapers and magazines were being sold on lurid, negative stories of the innocent-looking girl from Seattle who had been caught up in the elements of sex, drugs and murder, and insinuated – when they did not say it outright – that Amanda had all of her friends and family hoodwinked and that she had been leading a double life. Whether or not this was accurate, of course, remained to be seen, but one has to pause and wonder how much of the negativity that surrounded Amanda had been brought on by herself through her own behaviour and actions.

Take, for instance, a shopping trip that occurred on November 3, the day after Meredith's body had been found. According to information that was reported to the police and made its way into the international press, Amanda and Raffaele were seen at a popular discount store in Perugia called Bubbles, purchasing women's undergarments. The store's owner later said that he had heard Raffaele whisper to Amanda, 'We can have wild sex tonight. *Sesso selvaggio.*'

Amanda's father, Curt Knox, who works as a manager at Macy's store in Seattle, later told *Radar* magazine that the underwear story was ridiculous. He said that he travelled to Perugia to retrace her movements that day, and found that the only reason Amanda had gone into the store to buy underwear was because she had no clothing to wear – the cottage where she had resided had been sealed off by the police since Meredith's death. He also claimed that music played inside the store is so loud that no one 'could hear anything that anybody says'.

Because of the media's characterization of Amanda, her family naturally went on the defensive early on in an effort to show that she was not this unbalanced young woman, capable of committing a heinous crime. Her father referenced the date rape story that the media culled from her MySpace page and told reporters that when she had been given the writing assignment by her instructor she had been told to 'visualize a crime'. Curt Knox charged that the media had taken small details from her life and had 'created someone who was 180 degrees from anybody we had ever known. They've created a person who does not exist.'

Her family also cited a much-published photograph of her, taken from her MySpace page, depicting Amanda dressed all in black – dress pants, a long-sleeved black top, and black high-heels – in a pose with her right leg up on a piano bench, her right arm extended and resting on her knee. While some accounts referred to the photograph as provocative, even promiscuous, her family explained that it was taken by Amanda's 19-year-old younger sister, Deanna, for a photography class.

'So, basically the perception that the media is using, that this is a provocative image, that's a school assignment for her sister,' Curt Knox said.

But from that point forward, it seemed, partly because of Amanda's perceived coldness and lack of emotion concerning the murder of her flatmate on All Saint's Day, the media – as well as the police – used the perception to not only incriminate her in the murder but to convict her in the so-called 'court of public opinion'. The lovey-dovey scenes snuggling up to and kissing Raffaele were reproduced and spread through the media like wildfire, and reports of her doing cartwheels in the police station, and going out for pizza after Meredith's murder, were all used to vilify her. Others, however, were left wondering that rather than being cold and unfeeling, she was merely expressing an immature nature. Some newspapers speculated whether she had been somehow damaged by living in the rainy Pacific Northwest, which is more often than not damp and darkly overcast, and she seemed unable to escape the unflattering characterization of *'una cacciatrice d'uomini, insaziabile a letto'* (a huntress of men, insatiable in bed), in the Italian media.

Although it appeared that things could not get much worse for Amanda and Raffaele, the media frenzy surrounding the case took a new turn when photographs, taken from a blog site of Raffaele's, emerged and were quickly snapped up and published by the tabloids. One photo depicted the doctor's son dressed as a surgeon holding a large meat cleaver in one hand and a bottle of bleach in the other. Although it was not clear when or where the photographs were taken, an entry on his site described trips he had taken to Prague, Nuremburg, and the Nazi concentration camp known as Dachau. The images and stories appeared less than a week after Meredith's murder.

In his blog, Raffaele described himself as Christian, 'very honest, peaceable, sweet but sometimes totally creazy [sic]'. He also said that his favourite sport was kick-boxing. During that first week after Meredith's murder, Raffaele also spoke publicly about her, telling a journalist how he and Amanda had 'discovered' Meredith's blood-soaked body.

'It is something I hope to never see again,' he said. 'There was blood everywhere and I couldn't take it all in. My girlfriend was her flatmate and she was crying and screaming, "How could anyone do this?"'

Reportedly very composed, Raffaele also said that Meredith was always smiling and seemed perpetually happy. He said that Meredith was 'really popular' with students and other people her age, and that it was 'horrible that someone would want to hurt her'.

He described how he and Amanda had gone to a party with friends the night Meredith was killed, and that they had returned to his apartment, located in an old building on a steep, curvy hillside street, where they spent the night. Amanda, he said, returned to the villa she shared with Meredith and the other girls around lunchtime the following day to take a shower.

'When she arrived the front door was wide open. She thought it was weird, but thought maybe someone was in the house and had left it ajar. But when she went into the bathroom she saw spots of blood all over the bath and sink. She ran back to my place because she didn't want to go into the house alone. I agreed to go back with her.'

He said that when they walked into the flat together a short time later, he knew right away, in part due to the eerie silence, that something was wrong.

'The bathroom was speckled with blood,' he said, 'like someone had flicked it around. Just little spots. We went into Filomena's bedroom and it had been ransacked, like someone had been looking for something. But when we tried Meredith's room, the door was locked. I tried to knock it down but I wasn't strong enough so I called the police.'

The police, however, had noted that the call made from Raffaele's phone purportedly to notify them of his and Amanda's discovery had been made after officers had already arrived. He went on to describe how he followed officers into Meredith's room.

'It was hard to tell it was Meredith at first, but Amanda started crying and screaming,' he said. 'I dragged her away because I didn't want her to see it, it was so horrible. It seems the killer came through the window because it was smashed and there was glass all over the place.'

In the hours and days that followed, the inconsistencies in the accounts provided by Amanda and Raffaele would be noted, even pointed out to the media, and the once charming couple would be even more vilified, correctly or not, in the eyes of all those who were so closely following their case around the world.

Among the points that were made public was the fact that Amanda had broken down during questioning by police when she told of hearing Meredith screaming, when Lumumba purportedly had gone into Meredith's room. That, of course, was in direct conflict with Raffaele's account in which he had backed Amanda's claims of having spent that Thursday evening together.

If Amanda had taken Lumumba that evening to the house she shared with Meredith, she could not possibly have spent the entire night with Raffaele. When confronted with the discrepancy, Raffaele told the police that he had, in fact, been at home alone during the evening hours and that Amanda had joined him at 1 a.m.

So who was telling the truth, the police wondered. Was anyone connected to the case being truthful?

Lawyers for Amanda and Raffaele – Luciano Ghirga and Tiziano Tedeschi, respectively – were naturally outraged that Amanda's statement to the police was leaked to the *Corriere Della Sera*, and came out publicly, in an obvious effort to counter the damage that had already been done, by proclaiming their innocence.

Ghirga said that Edda Mellas, Amanda's mother and a maths teacher in the U.S., 'is convinced her daughter is innocent.' He also said that 'we maintain her innocence.' Similarly, Tedeschi said that his client, Raffaele, was at his home in Perugia on the night Meredith was killed.

'We believe he was online that night,' Tedeschi said. 'We are sure of Raffaele's innocence... we will show that at the time this [murder] was taking place, Raffaele was on his computer. He had nothing to do with this murder and is completely innocent... the possible hypothesis is, that being with a beautiful girl he allowed himself to be drawn into giving her an alibi.' Both lawyers agreed that Amanda and Raffaele had been 'lynched by the media'.

Although Amanda's mother was not allowed to see her daughter until Saturday, visiting day, she was provided with an apartment to use by the Perugia council – an unusual kindness. 'The council has provided her with an apartment for the time that she is in the city,' Paolo Occhiuto said. 'We feel that it is only fair and civilized to offer her some hospitality while she is in Perugia – it is the human thing to do.' Interestingly, Perugia is twinned with Seattle, Washington – Amanda Knox's hometown.

Before the week was out the police publicly announced that they were examining a 'flick knife' with an 8.5 centimetre blade which they considered 'compatible' with the wounds to Meredith's throat. They said that they had found the knife in Raffaele's possession. Investigators also submitted documents to a judge that read, in part, that Amanda Knox 'has shown an unscrupulous tendency to lie repeatedly to investigators involving the young Sollecito in such a serious affair'.

Amanda, Raffaele, and Lumumba were kept in isolation throughout much of that first week of the investigation, and were not allowed to see family or friends.

'Ms Knox crumbled under questioning,' said Arturo De Felice, Perugia's police chief. 'The three are now in jail with a chance to reflect on the inconsistencies in their accounts.'

Although Judge Claudia Matteini said that she was postponing her decision on whether there was sufficient evidence to hold the three murder suspects for 24 hours pending further investigation, the police, including De Felice, considered the case closed.

CHAPTER 7

By Thursday, November 8, 2007, a number of people back home in the U.S. had begun questioning whether Amanda Knox, characterized, among other things, as a 'fresh-faced girl', had the capacity to commit, or even be involved in, a crime as heinous as the one that took Meredith Kercher's young life, or whether she was in fact a good person who had become swept up in something of which she was not fully cognizant. Most of the people who knew her did not believe that she would have participated in such a crime, yet much of what was being made public painted a picture of a young woman who many people believe may have been leading a double life.

Accusations in the media were inflammatory, to say the least, with screaming headlines such as *The wild raunchy past of Foxy Knoxy*, or *Inside the twisted world of flatmate suspected of Meredith's murder*.

Some publications stated that police believed that Meredith had actually been held down by Amanda as she was killed in a sex attack that allegedly involved Patrick Lumumba, and one newspaper in particular stated that Amanda had 'left an imprint of her fingers' on Meredith's skin, as stated earlier. Still others speculated that Amanda's affinity for rock climbing had given her strong hands, sufficient strength to hold Meredith down, or worse. Others even suggested, and later charged, that Raffaele had held her down and that it had been Amanda who had wielded the knife.

If what was being stated in the media was accurate, many wondered how the various media sources had obtained the information. Were reporters embellishing the facts to sell newspapers or scoop the headlines on the evening news? Or was the information in fact being leaked to media sources in conspiratorial fashion to help the police paint an unflattering picture of the young couple, to aid them in moving their case along?

At one point the papers somehow obtained extracts from a letter that Raffaele Sollecito had written to his father – Dr Francesco Sollecito, a prominent urologist – from jail, in which he had expressed his thoughts about Amanda.

'I thought she was out of this world,' Raffaele had written. 'She lived her life like a dream; she was detached from reality... The Amanda I know is an Amanda who lives a carefree life. Her only thought is the pursuit of pleasure at all times.'

The pursuit of pleasure at all times? What exactly did that mean, or entail? Again, people wondered whether this thought of pursuing pleasure had clouded her judgment the night Meredith was killed.

As the investigation continued, detectives interviewed Sophie Purton, 20, a friend of Meredith's and a fellow student, who told them that Meredith had shared with her information indicating that Amanda had brought a number of men back to the villa. Purton was just one of several student friends of Meredith's that detectives would interview over the course of the investigation.

'Meredith told me that Amanda brought men back to their house,' Purton said. 'I don't know how many. Meredith told me in particular about one man who lives in an internet café. Meredith thought this man was very strange.'

In just about any investigation conducted in near fever-pitch intensity, such as this one, detectives would have been all over the lead about the man who lives in an internet café. They would want to know his name, his background, whether he was connected to the victim or the suspects (or both), whether he had an alibi for the night of the murder, and so forth. But the lead, although duly noted, seemed to go by the wayside as investigators seemed certain that they already had in custody those they believed responsible for Meredith's death. After all, most of the police – including Perugia's chief of police – already considered the case closed.

Murders are frequently, even typically, solved – at least in part – by determining the motive. Sometimes the motive remains a mystery. In this case, officials ranging from police to forensic pathologists had said they believe Meredith's murder had been violently sexually motivated. Considering the circumstances surrounding her death, that seems to be a given. Based on the nature and number of the knife wounds to her neck, the case also looked like a torturous, violent sex game that had gone too far and had been played against the will of the victim, and that she had been allowed to die over a lengthy period, so that the identities of those who had attacked Meredith died with her. Indeed, some people close to the investigation speculated later that Meredith may very well have survived the attack had she obtained medical attention, but her killers, knowing that they could not allow Meredith to identify them, could not let that happen.

At various points as the investigation continued the team of detectives re-examined the crime scene video made on the day Meredith's body was found. It began outdoors, showing the exterior of the hillside cottage that Amanda and Meredith shared with the two other girls. It included shots of Amanda and Raffaele standing nearby, both of them chewing gum and exchanging glances. At one point Amanda could be seen, standing several feet away from Raffaele, mouthing a message to her boyfriend, but it was not

Meredith Kercher *(above left)* and Amanda Knox *(above right)* were both exchange students in Perugia, Italy, and rented rooms in the upstairs flat of a house on Via della Pergola *(below)*.

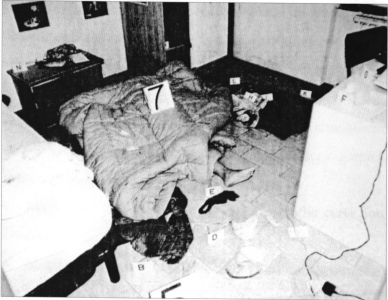

Above: A photo posted on Meredith's Facebook page of her at the Halloween party that she attended the night before she was murdered.

Below: On the morning of the 2nd November 2007, the local police made a gruesome discovery.

© *Olycom SPA/Rex Features*

Above: The murder made the front page of newspapers in Italy and around the world.

Below: Amanda Knox, pictured at the crime scene the day after Meredith's body was discovered.

© *Nick Cornish/Rex Features*

Above: Local bar owner Patrick Lumumba was falsely implicated by Knox and subsequently arrested. However, two weeks later he was freed and reunited with his wife and young son. He was later awarded compensation for unjust imprisonment.

© *Olycom SPA/Rex Features*

Below: Lumumba's defence lawyer speaking to the press.

© *Olycom SPA/Rex Features*

Above: 20 year-old Rudy Guede, whose DNA was all over the crime scene, is escorted by Italian police after fleeing to Germany after the murder.

© *Olycom SPA/Rex Features*

Below: Amanda Knox *(left)* was arrested on suspicion of murder on 6th November 2007, along with her then boyfriend, Raffaele Sollecito *(right)*. The press has largely focused on the role of Amanda Knox and, as a result, Sollecito remains somewhat of a mystery to the general public.

© *Nick Cornish/Rex Features & Olycom SPA/Rex Features*

Above: Meredith's sister Stephanie, mother Arline and father John at a press conference in November 2007.

Below: The funeral took place on 14th December 2007 in Croydon, Surrey. The church was packed with mourners at this private service, a testament to how popular Meredith was. © *Ray Tang/Rex Features*

Above: Rudy Guede opted for a 'fast-track' trial and was found
guilty of murder in October 2008.   © *EPS/Rex Features*

Below left: Knox looks at Sollecito during their trial in June 2009.
                                                    © *Olycom SPA/Rex Features*

Below right: Curt Knox and his ex-wife Edda Mellas, Amanda's
mother and father, leaving their lawyer's office in Perugia.
                                                    © *Arnold Slater/Rex Features*

Knox and Sollecito, pictured at the trial on 3rd December, 2009.
The next day they were sentenced to 26 and 25 years respectively.

© Olycom SPA/Rex Features

immediately known what she was attempting to convey to him.

The video then moved into Meredith's bedroom, where disturbing footage was captured of her bloodied face with her eyes open; another shot showed a foot protruding from a duvet on the bloodstained floor. The video also showed Meredith's bra lying on the bedroom floor, and blood on the bedroom door handle. At one point the duvet was pulled back to reveal Meredith's bruised and semi-naked body.

The footage also captured the blood in the adjoining bathroom, including blood on one of the tap handles. Forensic investigators were filmed as they examined bloody footprints and fingerprints, including a bloody handprint on the wall in Meredith's bedroom and a handprint on her pillow. However, only one of Amanda's fingerprints was found – on a kitchen glass – backing the police theory that the cottage had been cleaned after Meredith's death.

The video also showed a large rock lying beneath a desk in Filomena Romanelli's bedroom, which police believed was used to break the window in Meredith's room in an attempt, they would say, to make the attack appear as if it had been carried out by a burglar.

By this point in the investigation another pathologist, Dr Mauro Bacci, concurred with earlier findings that Meredith's killers had attempted to strangle her before stabbing her in the throat. There seemed to be some disparity of opinion, however, regarding the size of the knife used in the slaying. The postmortem examination revealed that the fatal wound to her throat had possibly been caused by a penknife and that judging by the depth of the wound, was likely to have been made by a man.

Meanwhile, the flick knife taken from Raffaele, who admitted he was a knife collector, had been found inside a pocket of his jeans. He told detectives that he always carried the knife with him. Investigators early on had decided that the flick knife was probably not the murder weapon, but a second knife, the type and size of which was not described, was found outside, in the garden of Raffaele's apartment. Yet another knife was recovered from Raffaele's kitchen. Forensic testing, including examination for fingerprints and DNA, was carried out on all of the knives, and it was determined that both Meredith and Amanda's DNA was found on the knife from Raffaele's kitchen.

When questioned about how this could be possible, Raffaele reportedly said that he had accidentally cut Meredith with the knife when he, Amanda and Meredith had been cooking together at the cottage. When pressed for more information about the knives and why he carried such weapons with him, Raffaele repeated that he was a collector and had a longstanding fascination with knives and weaponry.

When police searched Raffaele's apartment they had smelt bleach, leading them to believe that he had attempted to clean a knife or knives, as well as other items. Police also claimed that someone had made a Google search for 'bleach' and 'blood' on Raffaele's computer the morning after the murder, and under the circumstances had considered such a search highly suspicious. When combined with the earlier statement from store owner Marco Quintavalle, who had identified Amanda Knox as having come into his store to make purchases on the morning of November 2, and Raffaele's supposed fascination with extreme sex and the explicit Japanese *manga* comics, the evidence, albeit circumstantial, was becoming more damning.

A footprint made in blood found earlier in Meredith's bedroom was not helping Raffaele's case, either. One of a pair of sneakers owned by Raffaele seemed to match the bloody imprint.

Despite the evidence that apparently pointed to Raffaele's involvement in Meredith's murder, the Italian and English media, however, seemed intent on focusing their attention on Amanda by insinuating, if not outright stating, that Raffaele was merely an unwitting dupe being unscrupulously 'played' by the attractive and manipulative Amanda. Amanda's family, however, including her sister, Deanna, insisted that Amanda was getting a raw deal and was being unjustly and unfairly vilified. They stated forcibly that she was not at all like she was being portrayed in the media.

'Amanda is the nicest person in the world,' Deanna said. 'She always puts others before herself, and I feel like I am involved with her drama... she was at the wrong place at the wrong time.' Deanna told reporters that she and her family had assisted Amanda in finding the cottage in Perugia.

'When we went to see the place, Amanda fell in love with it right away,' Deanna said. 'She especially loved the garden. Everyone thinks Amanda is some kind of praying mantis, but she is not like that. She has the ability to light up a room with her smile. She has a great heart.'

However, there was another side to Amanda that was being explored. While attending the University of Washington, Amanda, the young honors student, had been fined the equivalent of approximately £135 for involvement in a 'residential disturbance', the details of which were not revealed. She also wrote on her MySpace page of her German ancestry on her mother's side of the family in which she jokingly inferred that she was secretly a Nazi. The social networking site also showed a photo of Amanda holding an old machine gun during an apparent visit to Germany with a caption that read, *The Nazi on the inside*. Her friends, however, also stuck by her, insisting that she was not like the person being portrayed. One friend stated that she would be the last person anyone 'would have thought would get involved in something like this. She wasn't at all wild or promiscuous.'

Yet, by her own later admission in a diary she kept in jail but which was at one point leaked to the press, Amanda would purportedly mention in her *Spiderman*

2 notebook that she had a sexual history that involved five men. Two men, besides Raffaele, reportedly would tell authorities that they'd had sex with her during the short time that she had been in Italy, but it would be stated later in the London media that they admitted knowing Amanda but denied ever having sex with her. One of the two men, known as Juve, said that he had worked at Le Chic with Lumumba.

'We were friends,' Juve said. 'We met because she also worked at Le Chic. We sometimes danced salsa, but I have a girlfriend and nothing ever happened. I walked her home sometimes at night, but I didn't have sex with her.'

It was not clear whether the five men mentioned in her diary included the other two men that came forward with the information *and* Raffaele or whether they were *in addition* to the other two men and Raffaele.

Stefano Bonassi, a student who resided in the flat below Amanda and Meredith, told investigators that Amanda had sex with one of his friends. Aside from bolstering their theory regarding Amanda's purported sexual promiscuity and how that aspect of her life could be related to the case, Bonassi's statement did not seem to carry much weight with the detectives.

Had the combined fascination of sex between Amanda and Raffaele been the impetus that had propelled forward a sexually-motivated attack against Meredith? Many people, both from within and without the judicial system, pondered that and a number of other questions needed to be answered.

Her diary also purportedly placed additional suspicion onto Raffaele. In her writings, she questioned whether Raffaele may have crept out during the night and gone to the cottage to rape and kill Meredith and, upon his return, brought the murder weapon into contact with Amanda while she was sleeping.

Another question needing an answer focused on why Amanda had brought Lumumba home to the cottage with her if he 'scared' her, as she had claimed. It just did not seem to add up. And if she had in fact been scared of Lumumba, why hadn't others been? Nearly everyone who spoke to the police or the media portrayed him as a gentle person with a friendly personality. Had she merely made the claim to try to avert suspicion from her and Raffaele? And if so, how much of her statement implicating Lumumba could even be believed?

Later that same day, November 8, Judge Claudia Matteini, after reviewing the details of the case as they were so far known, ruled that there was 'sufficient evidence' to keep Amanda, Raffaele, and Patrick Lumumba in custody while the investigation continued. The judge's decision was based, at least in part, on her being told that Amanda 'has shown an unscrupulous tendency to lie constantly to investigators,' and that the police 'believe the attack last Thursday night may have followed a session of drug taking.' The prosecution also brought to the judge's attention the fact that 'toxicology tests are not yet complete but they [investigators] have found marijuana plants in the garden of the house.'

Matteini, in deciding which charges to level against the suspects, reportedly also considered the two differing accounts related to the police by Amanda, as well as the fact that police had been monitoring Amanda's mobile phone. The night before their pre-dawn arrests, investigators purportedly heard Amanda telling Raffaele, 'I cannot do it any more, I cannot bear it.' It was becoming a question of who was actually at the scene of the murder, who did what afterwards, and now who was protecting whom?

In the meantime, lawyers for the three suspects continued to insist that each was innocent. Raffaele's lawyer said that Raffaele was at home when Meredith was killed, despite the allegations being made by the police that he and Amanda had broken a window at the cottage and ransacked the rooms to stage a break-in.

Luciano Ghirga, Amanda's lawyer, defined the case as 'strange and dramatic,' and said prior to Matteini's ruling to continue holding the suspects that 'we have applied for our client to be released on the grounds that she has nothing to do with this.'

Similarly, Carlo Pacelli, Lumumba's lawyer, said that 'Patrick was not involved in this at any time.' Pacelli said that Lumumba never 'entered the house of horrors because he was at his place of work.' He said that receipts from Le Chic's till would back up the fact that Lumumba was at work when the murder occurred.

By this time, barely a week into the investigation of Meredith's murder, it was difficult to tell who was lying outright or who was covering up for whom. The case seemed destined to be built around lies and deceit, confusion, and sensational reporting in nearly every media source. Many began to wonder if the true facts of the case would ever be revealed.

CHAPTER 8

By the following day, Friday, November 9, 2007, details of a report about the case by Judge Claudia Matteini – described as a meticulous woman in her mid-40s with a reputation for scrupulous attention to detail – began to emerge. Her report stated, in part, that with the door to Meredith's room open after investigators knocked it down 'there was a chilling scene in so far as the room was found in disorder with bloodstains everywhere, on the ground and on the walls, and also under the duvet of the bed a foot could be seen.' The report stated how police, in an effort to avoid contamination of the crime scene, had 'stopped everyone from entering the room.'

The report was part of her ruling in which she had decided that the police could hold the three suspects for up to a year while the investigation continued, because there were 'serious indications of guilt' that warranted such a decision. She also expressed concern that any or all of the suspects might flee the area or the country in an effort to avoid the investigation and subsequent prosecution, or that they might repeat the crime with another victim, and cited her concern as reasons for keeping the suspects in custody.

Matteini's report described how a 'girl, found dead with a blow to her neck with a sharp weapon, was identified as Meredith Kercher,' and that Dr Luca Lalli, the pathologist who conducted the first postmortem examination of the body, had 'established that the death occurred at 11 p.m. at the earliest and at the latest one hour after the… scope of a time-frame between 10 p.m. and midnight' on November 1, 2007. Also included was Lalli's professional opinion that Meredith had died due to a 'haemorrhage from a neck wound' following the 'blow of a sharp and pointed weapon.'

Lalli's notes also stated that 'bruises and lesions found on the neck suggest that Meredith was held by the neck leaving bruising compatible with the pressure of fingers,' and that she had been 'subsequently threatened with a knife held to her throat sufficient to leave other small wounds beyond those which determined death.' Lalli's report also showed that Meredith's death was likely to have been agonizingly slow because her carotid artery had not been cut, leaving her to bleed out at a much slower rate than if it had been severed.

'The fact that Meredith was a victim of violence is

evident from the state in which her body was found,' Matteini's report stated. 'There were bruises, particularly as mentioned in Dr Lalli's report where there is evidence of bruising with dark areas on the lips, and also on the gums of the left cheek and chin.'

Matteini also revealed information indicating that Meredith had a boyfriend, Giacomo Silenzi, 22, who resided with three other young men on the ground floor of the cottage where she lived. Investigators had ruled them out as possible suspects because they provided alibis for their whereabouts at the time of Meredith's murder. The young men, as well as Amanda and Meredith's two roommates, had left on the eve of *Il Giorno dei Morti*, the *Day of the Dead*, a national Italian holiday in which families throughout Italy visit the graves of their relatives. As a result, no one was in the cottage to hear Meredith's screams or her cries for help, except for Meredith and her killer or killers.

Silenzi, police learned, had met Meredith through Amanda Knox two months earlier and they had begun dating. A guitar player in a punk rock band, Silenzi said that he had fallen in love with Meredith. Silenzi said that he was friends with both Lumumba and Raffaele, and that Amanda often came to visit him at his flat where they listened to music and played the guitar. He said that Amanda was a Beatles fan, and she had expressed interest in wanting to 'learn to play (the guitar) properly.' After giving her a few lessons, Silenzi said that Amanda began bringing Meredith along with her.

'From the beginning we were very close, and we quickly decided to go out,' Silenzi said. 'We went to a disco where we kissed for the first time and then we went to my place and slept with each other. Our relationship grew stronger and stronger every day.'

It was established that Silenzi was out of town with family members the day that Meredith was killed, and he was subsequently cleared of any involvement in her death.

The report also stated that during interviews with the police, Filomena Romanelli, one of Meredith's flatmates, said that Meredith and Amanda appeared to be close and had spent a lot of time together – they typically accompanied each other to the university, and hung out within the same circle of friends. Filomena was insistent in her statements to the police that Meredith never allowed any male visitors into her bedroom except for her boyfriend.

The report pointed out inconsistencies in statements made by Amanda and Raffaele, and indicated that the couple was the primary focus of the investigation. The police discovered, for example, that Amanda had not called the police to investigate a break-in at the cottage, as she had stated to the postal police, who had already arrived to return the mobile phones found in the neighbour's garden, but had called the Carabinieri only *after* the Postal Police had arrived. As a result of the alleged deception, investigators now believed that Amanda and Raffaele had 'wished it to be thought they had been surprised outside the building where the murder was carried out.'

Another inconsistency pointed out by Matteini concerned the toilet in one of the bathrooms, which Amanda had said contained faeces. Raffaele, when interviewed by the police, had confirmed Amanda's account of the day's events except 'that he found the water in the toilet clean,' without faeces.

'However, when the military police [Carabinieri] arrived, the water [in the toilet] was found to be still dirty with faeces,' stated the report. Why was there a difference in their stories? Had Raffaele forgotten what Amanda had said about the faeces? Or had he not known about her statement?

When Matteini's report addressed Lumumba's alleged involvement in the murder: it said that he had claimed to have opened Le Chic at 'around 5 or 6 p.m.', and that his statement did not match information and evidence obtained by the police; it stated that Lumumba had changed his mobile telephone immediately the day after the murder; it contained information of how the police believed that Amanda had arranged a meeting between Meredith and Lumumba; it also laid out a theory about Raffaele's involvement on the night of the murder.

'Raffaele Sollecito,' the report stated, 'bored with the same old evenings, and desiring to try out strong sensations, went out with Amanda and met Lumumba at Piazza Grimana at 9 p.m. It was roughly at this same time that Sollecito and Knox both switched off their mobile phones until the following morning.

'A short while later Meredith returned – or she could have already been there – [and] went into her bedroom with Patrick after which something went wrong, in a sense that Sollecito with every probability also intervened and the two began to make advances which the girl refused. She was then threatened with a knife, the knife which Sollecito generally carried with him and which was used to strike Meredith in the neck. The three, realizing what had happened, quickly left the house, creating a mess with the intention of simulating a break-in, spreading blood everywhere and in an attempt to clean up, left drops of blood in the bath, on the ground and in the sink.'

Matteini said that it was not clear yet who may have inflicted the fatal stab wound, but indicated that it was not looking good for any of them – especially Raffaele, whose footprints investigators claimed were found inside Meredith's bedroom, and the fact that investigators believed the murder weapon was a knife with an 8.5 cm blade. According to forensics experts, 'three shoe imprints were found under the duvet that covered Meredith's body,' but only one of them was clear enough to yield useful results as it turned out to be 'compatible in shape and size with the sole of shoes confiscated from Raffaele Sollecito.'

Furthermore, Amanda, in her meetings with prosecutors, had outright accused Lumumba of killing

Meredith despite having 'confused memories', having smoked hashish with Raffaele in the afternoon. Nonetheless, a portion of Matteini's 19-page ruling/report claimed that Amanda had told prosecutors that Patrick had 'slipped off with Meredith... on whom he had a crush... in the bedroom, where they had sex... she added that she could not remember if Meredith had been previously threatened but that it was Patrick who killed her. She made clear that in those moments... she heard Meredith scream so much that she, being scared, covered her ears.'

When reporters began questioning the fact that Amanda had provided differing accounts of what had occurred the night Meredith was killed, and questioned the validity of her accusations against Lumumba, her lawyer, Luciano Ghirga, said that he had warned Amanda against making unfounded accusations. Regarding her inconsistent accounts of the events, he said that 'it is difficult to evaluate which one is true.'

'We told her that it would be worse than assassination to accuse an innocent person,' Ghirga said. 'We explained to her what slander means in Italy, so we'll see.'

Ghirga also said that Amanda's parents would be visiting her on Saturday, and he hoped that 'they will impress upon her the importance of telling the truth and clearing up the facts.'

Luca Maori, one of Raffaele's attorneys, said that

he would appeal the judge's decision to keep his client in custody. Maori said that he hadn't expected the ruling, and was 'perplexed' by the judge's decision.

Lawyer Tiziano Tedeschi, also representing Raffaele, said that despite the fact that forensics experts had identified an 8.5 cm knife belonging to his client as being compatible with the murder weapon, there was nothing to link Raffaele's knife with the wounds on Meredith's body. Tedeschi said that the wounds could have been inflicted by a common knife such as that used in the garden or in the kitchen. The suspected murder weapon was the knife taken from Raffaele after his arrest.

'If he killed Meredith,' Tedeschi said, 'he wouldn't exactly have taken it [the knife] into the police station when he was questioned.'

Despite the judge's decision to keep all three suspects locked up, it was revealed within the same time-frame of Matteini's ruling that forensic reports had so far not provided any evidence that Lumumba was ever inside Meredith's bedroom – in fact, at that point there was no evidence to show that he had ever been inside the cottage that was being dubbed the 'House of Horrors'. Out of 120 fingerprints obtained from inside the cottage, 40 were matched to the residents and people known to visit the cottage regularly, and the remaining 80 prints were listed as belonging to 'unknown individuals'. None of the fingerprints belonged to Lumumba, yet he remained in custody.

Before that Friday ended, a new bizarre and chilling twist was revealed as having occurred within the parameters of this already bizarre and chilling case. A shop assistant in Rome, Mauro Palmieri, came forward and told police that he had received an unusual text message on his mobile phone on the morning of October 31, the day before Meredith was killed. The text message had read: 'As far as I'm concerned tomorrow or this evening Meredith dies.'

Although he had been somewhat taken aback by the unusual message, Palmieri said that he assumed that he had received it by mistake and had deleted it because it had not meant anything to him. However, he said that 'it was quite a shock' when he had heard about Meredith's death a few days later. He said that he reported the message to the Carabinieri in Rome, who eventually passed the information to the police investigating Meredith's murder in Perugia. When questioned, Palmieri said that he had no connection with any of the individuals involved in the case and stated that he had only been to Perugia once in his life – 25 years ago during a school outing.

Investigators indicated that they would try to retrieve the message by examining massive quantities of cell phone data in an effort to determine if the message had been sent by any of the three suspects, but it appeared doubtful that they would be successful.

Meanwhile, John and Arline Kercher, back home in the UK, were awaiting the return of Meredith's body.

The necessary bureaucratic paperwork for the release of her body had been completed, signed by a judge, and arrangements had been made to fly it back that weekend, a little more than a week after her tragic and untimely death. The Kercher family could, perhaps, then take some solace from knowing that Meredith was coming home.

CHAPTER 9

On Saturday, November 10, 2007, following a visit to see her daughter in Capanne prison, just outside Perugia, Amanda's mother, Edda Mellas, at first had little to say about the reunion, issuing a curt 'no comment'. Hours later, however, it was being reported in the news media that Amanda had changed her story yet again by allegedly telling her mother during their meeting that she was not, in fact, present in the cottage when Meredith was killed. After having first told the Italian police that she had spent the entire evening with Raffaele Sollecito that night, Amanda later told investigators that she had been at the cottage and implicated Patrick Lumumba in the murder. Now, it seemed, she had reverted back to her original story.

Which of Amanda's accounts of that evening were true? Were any of her statements truthful?

'What my client is saying is that she is sticking to her

first version of events, that she was never there,' her lawyer, Luciano Ghirga, said. 'She has told her mother that she was not there when Meredith was there and that she was not even at the house but at the home of her boyfriend. The mother said that Amanda had told her she had said some stupid things the last few days and that she had made some wrong declarations. She told her mother that she was not even in the house and that she spent the night in question elsewhere and that this will help prove her innocence.'

Mellas told reporters after her visit with Amanda that her daughter was 'confident that she will be released soon.'

'Amanda is innocent of this and is devastated by the death of her friend,' Mellas added. 'She is completely distraught. We are not able to say anything else and are just letting the process follow its course... I saw my daughter for an hour, and I feel happier for having seen her.'

Despite the changes to her story in this latest instance in which she had essentially withdrawn her claim of having seen Lumumba enter Meredith's room that night, Italian police were nonetheless adamant that Patrick Lumumba was somehow involved in the murder and refused to release him.

His lawyer, Giuseppe Sereni, had filed a challenge to a portion of Judge Matteini's report in which Matteini had written that Meredith could have been killed as early as 9 p.m., shortly after returning home from her visit with friend Sophie Purton. Lumumba, however, continued to insist that he had been at Le Chic that evening, and had produced a series of time-stamped receipts from the till that began at 10.29 p.m.

In spite of his claims, *La Stampa* reported that police had conducted traces of Lumumba's mobile phone that placed him in an area of Perugia away from his bar at 8.38 p.m. The phone trace instead had placed him in an area of town that was in the vicinity of the cottage where Meredith lived.

Lumumba, meanwhile, insisted that there were witnesses who could place him at Le Chic during the time-frame in which Meredith was murdered, including a number of Belgian students who had been drinking there from 10.30 p.m. to 11.30 p.m. Lumumba's friends had begun spreading the word that anyone who had seen him at Le Chic that evening should come forward and tell the police.

Lumumba claimed that there had also been a visiting professor from Switzerland who had been at the bar from about 8.30 p.m. onwards. Hopeful that the Swiss professor could support Lumumba's alibi, Sereni and his staff were making a diligent effort to locate him.

'We think he is back in Zurich and we are searching,' Sereni said.

One of the reasons why investigators did not believe Lumumba's story was because he had said that he opened Le Chic between 5 p.m. and 6 p.m. the evening Meredith was killed, but a witness came forward claiming that he had seen that the bar was closed at 7 p.m. Based on the food content in Meredith's stomach, noted during the autopsy, police were now saying that she had died between 9 p.m. and 11 p.m. with the fatal wound inflicted about 30 minutes before she succumbed. With the phone trace placing Lumumba in the vicinity of the cottage at 8.38 p.m., investigators still believed that he could have killed Meredith and made it back to Le Chic by 10.29 p.m., in time to print out the first receipt he presented to support his alibi for the evening.

In yet another shocking aspect to the case, Lumumba's legal team petitioned a judge to prevent Meredith's body from being returned to Britain as her family waited for its arrival. The coffin that contained her body, already in a holding facility at an airport in Rome for the flight home, was prevented by the petition from being loaded onto a plane and was kept at the airport for several hours while a decision was being made. Lumumba's attorney, Sereni, cited crucial discrepancies over the time of Meredith's death as the primary reason for filing the petition. He also asked for a new autopsy.

'We want a new examination of Kercher's body because the original autopsy suggested her death could have been as late as midnight,' Sereni said. 'In the final report, the time of death is brought forward.'

Thankfully – for the sake of Meredith's family –

Lumumba's petition was denied in a reasonably short time and Meredith's body was flown home the following day. Relieved that his daughter's body had been returned, John Kercher told reporters: 'Now at least we can make the appropriate arrangements and we hope to have a funeral in a couple of weeks. We have been shocked by the stories about how she died – it is difficult, and we just want to get through this. We are taking it one day at a time.'

Meanwhile, it transpired that Kercher had apparently informed Italian prosecutor Giuliano Mignini that Meredith had told him that Amanda was entertaining men within a week of her arrival in Italy, and that Meredith had characterized her as 'eccentric' and 'sure of herself'. He told Mignini that his last conversation with Meredith had been only hours before her death, at about 3 p.m. on November 1. He related how they had only spent a couple of minutes talking because he did not want Meredith to spend a lot of money on phone charges.

'When we spoke she would always tell me about her day, what she had done, and about her friends,' Kercher said. 'She would always call in the evening when it was cheaper... when I heard an English girl had been murdered in Perugia I tried to call her but I couldn't get through at first. And then it just rang with no answer.'

The shocking characteristics of this bizarre case, however, with all of its twists and turns that had become somewhat confusing to many people attempting to follow the story, refused to end or go away. Shortly after the plane carrying Meredith's body left Rome for London's Heathrow airport, investigators had reportedly begun searching for a fourth suspect in Meredith's murder. The report of a bloody fingerprint found in her bedroom that did not match any of those of the three suspects had prompted investigators to renew their interest in, and subsequent search for, a North African man seen hastily washing clothes and a pair of trainers in a launderette the day after the murder. In addition to the fingerprint, the Italian press began reporting that DNA traces of the so-called 'fourth person' had been found in the bathroom of the cottage.

Was the new information another leak to the press? Was it reliable information? Because a fingerprint and DNA was involved it seemed as if it should be reliable information, but there were already so many aspects of the case that had become questionable. A member of the investigating team reportedly denied the new information by saying that the only 'mark' found in blood in Meredith's bedroom had been a footprint thought to be Raffaele's. The investigator confirmed that the man seen using the launderette was being sought for questioning, but in connection with another case.

Was the investigator telling the whole story? Or was his information comprised of partial-truths as an effort to protect any leads the investigating team might still be pursuing?

During this same time-frame, it was made known that Italian forensic experts had found strands of bloodied hair in Meredith's left hand and that they were being tested. The examination was being conducted on the hypothesis that Meredith had struggled with her attackers and had fought back, and in so doing may have grabbed onto a few strands of hair – damning evidence if it could be linked to someone by DNA.

Meanwhile, according to Father Saulo Scarabottoli, Amanda appeared to be 'shell-shocked' and had been 'writing page after page' about her feelings since being taken into custody. Scarabottoli, a chaplain at Capanne prison, had visited her daily since her arrest after she had been denied a request to attend Mass.

'Instead I visited her in her cell and explained to her the true sense of life and how values should be tied to moral behaviour,' Scarabottoli said. 'I told her that wild nights were a tragedy and she seemed to be listening very attentively to every word I said.' It appeared to Scarabottoli that Amanda was writing a prison diary.

'In the few moments I spent with her,' Scarabottoli said, 'it seemed she had a lot in her heart to think about, and I think she may be writing it down... she appeared to be a little overcome with her situation and seemed to be up and down. She didn't make any form of confession to me.'

The priest's comments seemed to confirm earlier reports that Amanda was keeping a diary. She reportedly had also told Franco Zaffini, an Italian politician who had visited Amanda, Raffaele and Lumumba, that she was 'grieving' over what had happened to Meredith, but insisted that she 'was not involved'.

'She said to me, "I am very sorry for what happened to my friend Meredith, but I had nothing to do with it,"' Zaffini said, adding, as an apparent afterthought, that Amanda had not asked him about Raffaele during his visit with her.

The next day, in yet another somewhat surprising development, and ironically immediately after she had changed her story again by telling her mother that she had not been at the cottage the night Meredith was murdered, police announced that CCTV cameras had recorded Amanda as she entered the cottage at 8.43 p.m. on the night of the murder – only a few minutes before Meredith herself came home after watching the movie with her friend. The CCTV cameras overlook the cottage from a nearby car park, and the recorded footage showed Amanda's face and light-coloured skirt and top. The footage clearly contradicted her latest claim that she was at Raffaele's house.

A police source, as reported in the media, said that: 'it will be interesting to see what she has to say when we show her the footage.' According to reports in the *Corriere Della Sera*, the CCTV images were very sharp.

It also came to light that Amanda had written a

letter to her mother barely three days after Meredith's murder asking her to take her shopping. Amanda apparently wrote the three-page letter after her Italian language course instructor asked the class to write something about their weekend. Among the things Amanda had written was that she was 'on edge' and could not 'stop thinking about Meredith's death'.

'What I really want, Mom, is for you to take me shopping,' she wrote. 'I haven't finished with Perugia, but I don't think I can go back to sleep in that house.'

In the meantime, Amanda Knox's statements and actions were believed to be helping the Patrick Lumumba defence team move a step closer to getting their client released from jail. Witnesses that placed him at work at Le Chic at the time of Meredith's murder were also coming forward, and it was only a matter of time before the Swiss professor would be located so that he could confirm or refute Lumumba's alibi. Helping his case even further was a statement from a porter who told police that he had gone to Le Chic to assist in repairing a drink dispenser – the porter said that he had seen Lumumba talking with a university professor on the night of the murder.

Things were not looking so good for Amanda and Raffaele, however.

CHAPTER 10

On her return to Britain following the terrible events in Perugia, Meredith's friend and fellow student Robyn Butterworth provided a statement to the police who forwarded it to the team of investigators in Perugia. Much of it centred on her observations of Amanda Knox and things that Meredith had said about her flatmate. At some point during the process, Robyn's statement was leaked to the press. Stating that Amanda was 'over the top' and 'strange', Robyn's statement included details of how Amanda appeared abnormally unfazed by what had happened to Meredith.

'I remember Amanda also kept going on about how she found the body,' Robyn said. 'It was as if she was proud to have been the one who found it.'

She recalled thinking while at the police station on Friday evening, November 2, the day Meredith's body was found, how Amanda's behaviour had seemed very strange, 'as if she wasn't bothered at all.' Her behaviour was also noticed by other friends who were there being questioned by investigators. She also told of how a group of those being questioned had assembled in the police waiting room, and that when she entered the room Amanda had been speaking loudly in English to everyone present.

'She described how she had come back to the apartment at around 11 a.m.,' Robyn said. 'She said that she had found the front door open, and that she had gone into the bathroom that she and Meredith shared. She was saying how she had seen blood on the floor. I remember her saying that it was menstrual blood. She also said she had taken a shower.'

Robyn recalled Amanda saying that the toilet 'was full of shit'.

'She kept saying the word "shit" over and over again,' Robyn added. 'This behaviour seemed a little strange to me.'

Robyn also told of how she had heard that Meredith argued with Amanda because Amanda never flushed the toilet after using it. It was a sore point with Meredith, and it had become somewhat confrontational. She said that Meredith had also told her about discussions that she'd had with Amanda about bringing men back to the cottage – a practice of which Meredith had not approved.

Even prior to that Friday evening inside the police waiting room, Robyn said that she had always considered Amanda strange, someone who appeared to be an extravagant type.

'I remember the first time we met,' Robyn said. 'We were in a restaurant having something to eat when all of a sudden she got up and started singing at the top of her voice. It was very strange and out of place.'

Robyn also revealed how she had been one of the last people to have seen Meredith alive. She had met up with her at the home of their mutual friend, Sophie Purton, early on Thursday evening, and all three girls had watched *The Notebook* together. Robyn's statement to the police corroborated other accounts, including Sophie's, namely that Meredith had left at approximately 9 p.m. to go home to bed.

Meanwhile, back in Italy, details of the prison visit between Raffaele and his father a day earlier began to emerge. His father expressed confidence that his son was innocent of involvement in Meredith's murder. His comments were brief, but seemed to centre on how Amanda had been responsible for bringing Raffaele into the situation.

'He is rather upset by the fact that a girl who he had only just met and who he treated so well has drawn him into this terrible episode,' Raffaele's father said. 'The sooner the truth comes out, then the sooner I can embrace my son again.'

Was Raffaele now blaming Amanda for getting him involved? It certainly seemed so as evidenced by his lawyer's comment.

'Raffaele doesn't talk about Amanda,' Luca Maori said. 'She has ruined his life.'

Despite the assertions of Raffaele's legal team that no traces of blood had been found on two knives seized from him by police, or on his trainers in which a bloody footprint had allegedly been made, it was revealed that investigators were in the process of examining his Audi car for signs of blood on the vehicle's pedals.

Investigators had already examined some of Raffaele's *manga* comic books with titles such as *Entitled Blood*, *Mad Psycho*, and *The Immortal*. Some of them were particularly violent, and seemed to glorify women being killed with swords and knives – one in particular depicted a woman who was killed on a bed. While he could not be convicted on his preference of reading material alone, possession of such material did nothing to help the case of the self-proclaimed knife collector.

Conducting interviews with the Italian media from his jail cell, Raffaele remained steadfast that he would be cleared of any involvement in Meredith's murder despite the mountain of evidence, circumstantial and otherwise, piling up against him. Describing himself as 'thoroughly honest,' he talked of returning to his studies when the case was over. One reporter asked him if he would do anything different if he could go back in time and change things.

'Yes, one thing,' he said. 'I wouldn't smoke joints

anymore. And then knives, I wouldn't carry one with me like I have so far.'

It was revealed that he had carried knives on his person since about the age of 13.

As he reflected on having spent the past week in jail, Raffaele said that he had spent his time reading books, writing and watching television. When a reporter asked him about Amanda Knox, he said that he never wanted to see her again.

'If I am here, it's her fault above all,' he said through his attorney. 'I am conscious that contrary to what I thought, our paths have diverged profoundly.'

When asked what he would like to say to Amanda, he responded: 'Nothing. I have absolutely nothing to say to her.'

Meanwhile, Lumumba's wife, Ola, broke her silence about her husband as the case entered its second week. She was in tears as she spoke about her husband: 'He is well and he has nothing to do with this. Patrick said to me that he was missing his friends, family and work... he strongly believes in justice, and I hope that in the next few days all this will be resolved... I just want my husband back – my baby and I are waiting for him at home.'

During this time-frame, officials at Capanne prison said that Amanda had been moved out of solitary confinement and into a cell with an older female inmate. The new cell was five metres by five metres and equipped with a cupboard, bathroom, kitchen area and a wardrobe. While not the comforts of home, the arrangement was considerably more than would typically be expected by a prisoner in a U.S. penal facility.

It was also reported that Amanda had found religion in jail, perhaps because of her contact with the chaplain and a number of nuns. Claiming that she was now a changed person, she said that she had previously been 'out of control' and that she 'bitterly regretted' her prior lifestyle. She said that there would be 'no more drugs and no more sex' if she was cleared in the case and got out of jail. She kept a copy of *The Gospel According to St. Mark* by her bed, and claimed to read from it every day. She reportedly had become fond of the adage, 'The future is what you make of it'.

By Thursday, November 15, 2007, specifics regarding the massive forensics tests began to appear in greater detail than had previously been reported, including additional information on the 7-inch, black-handled kitchen knife, initially said to have been seized from Raffaele's apartment. Although the police had previously said that it contained both Amanda's and Meredith's blood on it, they were being more specific now – Amanda's DNA had been found near the knife's handle, and Meredith's DNA had been found on the tip of its blade. However, investigators were now saying that they were unsure whether the knife came from Raffaele's kitchen or from the cottage that Amanda and Meredith had shared. They also said that it was not the knife that had been seized from Raffaele at the time of his arrest. The DNA finding was made by forensic scientists working in Rome, 100 miles south of Perugia.

'The DNA is a match for Amanda Knox and Meredith Kercher,' said Giacinto Profazio, who was involved in the investigation. 'It was DNA, not blood, which is very significant – and the DNA match for Meredith was on the top part of the blade, and the lower part, near the handle, was Knox's.'

The police also said that the knife in question had been cleaned with bleach. In fact, according to detectives, there were signs of bleach found all over Raffaele's flat, an indication to them that someone had meticulously cleaned his residence. A blood-soaked sponge had also been found there, and rags containing DNA from both Amanda and Raffaele had been found at the cottage where Meredith was killed.

At one point during the murder probe, Raffaele's underwear had been confiscated by police after spots of blood had been noticed. It was determined, however, that the blood belonged to Amanda and that it was probably menstrual.

When news of the DNA match found on the knife reached Raffaele, he never wavered, remaining steadfast that he was innocent of any wrongdoing. His legal team also continued to support his insistence that he had nothing to do with Meredith's murder.

As information about the bizarre case continued to

circulate from a variety of sources – some official, others not so official – on Sunday, November 18, Meredith's boyfriend, Giacomo Silenzi, spoke publicly about the case for the first time, recalling how he heard about Meredith's death.

'I was on a train heading back to Perugia from my parents' house when I got a call from Meredith's other flatmate, Filomena, who told me what had happened,' Silenzi told a reporter for the *Daily Mail*. 'My stomach dropped. I just could not believe it. I had spoken with her for the last time just a couple of days earlier and she had sent me a text saying she was looking forward to me coming back.'

He said that when he arrived at the Perugia train station, police picked him up and drove him to the police station. Describing Meredith as 'beautiful and innocent,' he said that he first suspected Amanda while they waited to be questioned by detectives at the police station on the day Meredith's body was found.

'I had a cast-iron alibi because I had been at my parents' house since the Monday [before the killing],' he said. 'It was a bank holiday in Italy. I was taken to a waiting room and Amanda was there.' He described how Amanda had hugged him and had told him how sorry she was about Meredith. She also introduced him to Raffaele, who Silenzi had never met before that day.

'I couldn't help thinking how cool and calm Amanda was,' Silenzi continued. 'Meredith's other English friends were devastated and I was upset, but Amanda was as cool as anything and completely emotionless. Her eyes didn't seem to show any sadness and I remember wondering if she could have been involved.'

Silenzi said that he had spoken with Meredith's British friends, Robyn Butterworth and Sophie Purton, that day, and they had offered similar feelings and opinions about Amanda. In fact, he said, none of them could understand how Amanda was able to deal with everything that had happened so calmly.

'I knew that Amanda didn't get on with Meredith,' Silenzi said, 'but I didn't think that would lead to Amanda killing her.' Tearfully, he described how he and Meredith had only just begun their relationship.

'Maybe it was too early to talk about love,' he said, 'but we really had an affection for each other. She moved into the flat above mine at the end of summer, and we would pop into each other's places just to say hello or have a cup of coffee, the things that neighbours do. She was very pretty, and I was also impressed with her Italian. We would share CDs and play music together.'

He said that his birthday was at the end of September and that a party had been planned in honour of it. Meredith, however, had been unable to attend because she was flying back to England to spend the weekend with her family.

'She gave me a bottle of rum as a present,' he said. 'Most of it was drunk at the party, but there is a drop left that I will now keep forever... a few weeks after that, around the middle of October, we kissed for the first time at a student party. Then we made love a couple of days later in my flat.

'I'm still having trouble taking this all in,' he continued. 'If I could see Amanda, I would just ask her, "Why? Why did she kill Meredith?"' Silenzi added that he had not been in touch with Meredith's parents, but indicated that he would like to attend her funeral and meet them, and then say goodbye to her.

As the second week of the investigation came to a close, a judge ruled that additional tests should be conducted to establish the exact time of Meredith's death, in response to a request by Lumumba's attorneys. These could involve another autopsy. The new development was the result of evidence from Lumumba's legal team. His lawyers apparently had found several witnesses who could place him at Le Chic at the time Meredith was killed.

Another revelation that pointed toward Lumumba's innocence had been DNA found on Meredith's body and in faeces that had been left in the toilet, neither of which matched Lumumba's DNA. The evidence, combined with the fact that Lumumba had never had even a minor infraction with the law, led people – including the police – to wonder if his arrest was in fact a horrible mistake. An American student, Allegra Morosani, who had studied for a semester in Perugia – and who had come to know Lumumba fairly well – said that Amanda's accusations against Lumumba had actually served to work against her in the court of public opinion.

'I was outraged that he had been considered a suspect,' the student said. 'Like, God, that bitch – how stupid of her to accuse him, because everyone would know that he couldn't have done it. He was the sweetest guy.'

Italian police, it seemed, may not have been entirely convinced themselves that Lumumba had been involved in the murder, because they had been working intently towards developing leads pointing toward a fourth suspect. Forensic investigators, it turned out, had discovered a bloody fingerprint on a pillow in the cottage where Meredith was killed, as well as another on a toilet-paper roll, neither of which had matched the three suspects already in custody. Although they were not saying much at that time, they did say that they believed the man being sought was of African origin and that he might be linked to selling drugs.

Because analysis of the fingerprints in question had been matched to 20-year-old Rudy Hermann Guede – a small-time drug dealer and petty thief who held dual citizenship from Italy and Cote d'Ivoire (the Ivory Coast) – reports identifying him as a suspect began circulating in Italy and wider afield. According to police, one of the fingerprints made in Meredith's blood had matched a fingerprint in Guede's file at the registry of foreign residents at Perugia's town hall. Investigators were not saying much about Guede except that an international warrant had been issued for his arrest, and that officers were closing in on him.

CHAPTER 11

By Monday, November 19, 2007 news reports about the international manhunt for Rudy Guede began to appear in the press and on television after it was revealed that police believe he left Perugia on the day that Meredith's body was found. Police were saying little at this point, only that they had matched one or more fingerprints left in Meredith's blood, and that Guede was suspected of participating in her sexual assault and murder. As police hunted for Guede across Europe, including France and Germany by some accounts, newspaper reporters were doing their own research to obtain as much information as they could about the new mystery man.

According to *La Repubblica* and other sources, Guede had moved to Italy with his father from the Ivory Coast when he was five. When his father returned to the West African country, Guede was taken in and raised by wealthy businessman Paolo Caporali and his family in Perugia. However, he proved to be rebellious, and the Caporali family had little to do with him after he had grown older. Although Guede had found work at a rural bed-and-breakfast, he eventually began to dabble in drugs as he started exploring Perugia's widespread student party scene.

'Guede was a difficult type,' said Simone Benedetti, a member of his adoptive family. 'He spent a lot of money, told lies, and did not behave well. If I had to judge him, I would say he was a boy who could not take care of himself. But no way is he a murderer.'

When he was about 16 he was injured during a knife fight over drugs, which left him with an abdominal scar. In time he became a well-known but small-time drug dealer and was referred to around town as 'The Baron'. He also became known as a petty thief.

At one point he moved to Milan for a while, but returned to Perugia a few days before Meredith was murdered. He had, in fact, been seen by a local barman walking in Perugia on Halloween night, and detectives began showing his photograph around the city's bars, with swift results. Pasquale Alessi, one of the owners of the Merlin pub, told police that Guede was a frequent visitor to another bar, the Domus nightclub where, investigators learned, Meredith had gone dancing the night before her death. But the potential connections between Guede and Meredith did not merely end at the Domus.

Police eventually learned that Guede had become friendly with the four men who shared the bottom half of the cottage where Meredith and Amanda resided, and was frequently seen at the Piazza Grimana basketball court, only a few metres away and on the route that the students habitually took to and from classes.

He apparently liked to play basketball at the open air court there, hence one of the reasons he liked to hang out at the dimly lit Piazza Grimana – the other being his involvement in illicit drugs, both in the capacity of their sale and usage. A list for a Perugia basketball team shows that Guede played guard in 2004 and 2005.

Rudy Guede also maintained a Facebook page, where he had posted photographs of himself in a number of Perugia bars. He listed his interests as 'arts, computers, basketball and girls'. Guede's Facebook page was still active after Meredith's death, with new message and posted entries. For example, on November 3 someone left Guede a message that read, 'You still in Perugia? I heard what happened with the English girl. Very crazy.' Another public message, also addressing Guede, asked, 'How are you doing in Sweden?'

In another development, after word began circulating about Guede being wanted by the police in connection with Meredith's death, another Perugian bar owner came forward and said that he had found

Guede in his house with a knife one night a few weeks before Meredith's murder. The bar owner, however, had declined to press charges against the intruder.

As the police continued their search for Guede, a disconcerting YouTube video of him materialized. Guede was obviously high on some illicit drug or substance when he made the video, as he continuously repeated, 'Oh my God. I'm an extraterra.' As the video continued, Guede rolls his eyes back and says, 'Oh mama, I'm a vampire, I'm Dracula. I'm gonna suck your blood.'

After learning that he was wanted by the police in connection with Meredith's murder, Guede apparently contacted the British *Guardian* newspaper via e-mail. He wrote: 'I didn't do nothing, but I won't talk with a policeman, 'cause I'm not a killer. See you in Perugia.'

Fortunately, the search for the African had not taken long to bring results and he was tracked to Germany through a friend – under police guidance – who had contacted him via the Internet. He and his friend chatted for several hours using Skype, with his friend, unknown to Guede, sitting in front of a computer at police headquarters as police listened in and passed him notes telling him what to say or which questions to ask.

'They are after you for the murder of Kercher,' said his friend, who the police declined to identify. 'What have you done?'

'I wasn't there that night,' Guede replied. 'If they

found my fingerprints, it must have been from before... I have been in the house. I knew Amanda and I knew Meredith, but I didn't kill her.'

The entire conversation, which lasted more than three hours, was monitored by the police. As a result, Italian police contacted German authorities and passed along information about Guede, including his photograph, and asked the Germans to be on the lookout for him.

At another point that same night Guede effectively did an about turn, telling another friend in an e-mail – also monitored by the police – that he had sex with Meredith on the night she was killed, but insisted that a stranger had killed her, not him. Guede explained during this e-mail exchange that Meredith had invited him to her bedroom on the night of November 1, and that they'd had consensual sex. He said that he had left her room to go to the bathroom and that while there he had heard the doorbell ring. Shortly afterwards, he said that he heard Meredith screaming from her room.

Guede claimed that he came out of the bathroom upon hearing Meredith's screams where he confronted a man that he could only describe as a 'brown-haired Italian'. He claimed that he scuffled with the man, and then fled the cottage after being injured. The e-mail exchange with the second friend clearly conflicted with the earlier Skype conversation in which he said that he was not there that night.

The results were swift, even though a bit of luck had been involved on the part of the police. Officers in Mainz, Germany, told Italian investigators that Guede had been arrested by transit police on Tuesday, November 20, after being detained on a train bound for Frankfurt. Apparently he had been caught travelling without a ticket, and he had no identification documents in his possession. He first gave officers a false name, and later attempted to claim political asylum, to no avail – it had not taken long for his true identity to surface. The German police in Germany said he would remain in custody while they checked for any outstanding warrants against him in their country and, if none were found, he would be returned to Italy within a matter of days, as long as he did not fight extradition.

Italian authorities were, naturally, elated over such a swift arrest and Arturo De Felice, Perugia's police chief, said that 'we had been in contact with our German colleagues for days,' and that Guede would be returned to Italy as soon as possible. The revelation by the police chief indicated that Italian police had known about Guede longer than had been indicated in the press. It was noted that none of the three suspects already in custody had ever mentioned Guede's name to police.

Although Guede's father said that he had not seen his son for more than a year, he believed he was innocent: 'Rudy was a lad who always loved others.

We all have faith in him. He cannot be responsible for such an atrocious crime.'

Meanwhile, on the same day that German authorities had arrested Guede, it was announced by the Italian news agency ANSA that Patrick Lumumba had been freed from jail due to lack of evidence. His release came about with little advance public notice and just as little fanfare, but after being held in jail for two weeks and unsure what the future held for him, Lumumba expressed his gratitude for the fact that all charges against him, pending or otherwise, had been dropped.

'I am happy to be going home... I very much thank God who had helped me to return home,' Lumumba said after his release. Later he would sue the police for 516,000 euros (about £458,000), for which an Italian court would eventually award him 8,000 euros (£7,100). He also began making plans to sue Amanda Knox for defamation of character and other damages.

After enjoying a night of freedom, Lumumba said the next day that he would never be able to forgive Amanda for falsely implicating him in Meredith's murder. 'I still don't understand how I finished up in all this,' Lumumba said. 'Because I'm black? Because I'm the perfect guilty one? Why didn't the police ask me anything before putting handcuffs on me? Why didn't they ask me where I had been that evening? Why didn't they investigate further? Why did Amanda blame me? I had offered her a job. I don't think I can forgive her.'

In yet another development, a preliminary forensic report leaked to the press showed that Raffaele Sollecito had not been using his computer on the night of the slaying, contrary to what he had claimed. An examination of his computer showed that it had been switched on that night, but remained unused between 9.10 p.m. and 5.32 a.m. He had previously insisted that he was online that night and had hoped that he would be able to use that fact as an alibi.

'Nothing was downloaded or uploaded to suggest Internet activity that night,' said Edgardo Giobbi, a detective working with Rome's Serious Crime Squad that had been assisting Perugia investigators.

However, Emilio Lucchetta, a private investigator hired by Raffaele's lawyers, said that Raffaele's Macintosh computer and the type of web browser he used made it difficult to analyze and said that 'there was Internet activity' on Raffaele's computer 'between 6.27 p.m. and 3.33 a.m.'

In light of the fast-changing circumstances and the turns that the case was taking, particularly Lumumba's release and exoneration and Guede's apprehension in Germany, Amanda's and Raffaele's families held onto renewed hope that they might soon be released. But there were plenty of troubling issues that remained, as well as a new one: why hadn't either of them ever mentioned to the police that they knew Rudy Guede? All anyone could get out of Amanda regarding the new suspect was that she may have vaguely recognized

Guede, that she may have seen him associating with the downstairs neighbours. She insisted that she never knew his name.

On Wednesday, November 21, Rudy Guede made a courtroom appearance, in Koblenz, Germany, where he was brought before a judge. He claimed he was innocent, and that he had nothing to do with the crime. He also agreed that he would not fight extradition.

CHAPTER 12

In the aftermath of Rudy Guede's apprehension in Germany and Lumumba's release in Italy, investigators in Perugia kept going over Amanda Knox's so-called confession – one of her accounts of what had occurred on the evening of November 1. If she had gone back to the cottage she shared with Meredith after having spent the prior evening at Raffaele's flat and had seen the blood in the bathroom, why would she have gone ahead and taken a shower as she had claimed? There was, after all, a considerable amount of blood in the bathroom, judging from the crime scene photos, and Amanda had merely said that she had thought the blood was 'a bit strange.' But had it not been 'strange' enough to prevent her from taking a shower? The photos taken by investigators had, after all, depicted something that looked rather more than a woman's menstrual bleeding, which is what Amanda had claimed. Her statements, as they were re-examined, were beginning to give the appearance of being contrived. Her so-called memory issues, purportedly caused because she had smoked cannabis and hashish, also did not seem believable.

'I find it hard to remember these moments,' Amanda had said, 'but Patrick had sex with Meredith. I can't remember whether Meredith was threatened first. I remember in a confused way that he killed her. Patrick and Meredith went into Meredith's room while I stayed in the kitchen. I can't remember how much time they were in the room. I can only say that at a certain point I heard Meredith scream and, frightened, I covered my ears with my hands. Then I don't remember anything.'

She claimed that because Patrick Lumumba's name had been in her head during questioning, she had seen him in 'flashbacks' as the killer. 'I'm very confused,' she had said. 'My head is full of contrasting ideas and I know I can be frustrating to work with for this reason… all I know is I didn't kill Meredith, and so I have nothing but lies to be afraid of.'

Whose lies, the police wondered. Her own? Much of the time during questioning, Amanda's statements had been rambling and at times incoherent. 'There is something inside me which I believe to be true. But there is another possibility that could also be true and, honestly, I can't say with any certainty which one is correct. I am trying to work it out because I fear for myself... I know I did not kill Meredith. That is something I know for sure.'

What was it that she was trying to work out? The police wondered. A way to shift the blame or responsibility for what happened that night onto someone else? It certainly seemed that way to her interrogators. And if she was being truthful, why did she 'fear' for herself?

'I'm not sure of these things and I know that it is important to help my case, but the truth is I don't think we did very much,' she had said to officers.

What did 'I don't think we did very much' mean? Had that statement been difficult to discern because of the rambling manner of her comments? Or had it been some kind of Freudian slip that may have alluded to her and Raffaele's involvement in what had happened to Meredith?

'At this moment my head is full of contrasting ideas and I don't like being unable to figure them out,' she had said in the interrogation room.

It seemed a bit strange that Amanda could remember smoking pot and that she was certain that she had not killed Meredith while being unable to remember much of anything else that occurred that night. None of what she had done or was doing seemed to be helping her or Raffaele's case. It certainly had not helped her when she reverted back to her original story of not being there during the visit with her mother.

'I stick by what I said originally,' she had maintained during the prison visit. 'I wasn't there. I'm innocent.'

As had been the case with many of the documents related to this investigation, Raffaele's jailhouse letter to his father was also leaked and made its way into the public domain before the third week of the police investigation was over. In it he seemed more in control about what he wanted to say, and his statements seemed more well thought out than anything that Amanda had said so far. He also accused Amanda of not being truthful in certain instances.

In the letter, Raffaele explained to his father that he had met Amanda at a concert, and that his first impression of her was that she was an interesting girl. He said that she looked at him 'over and over again' and 'seemed to be searching for something in my eyes, like a particular interest.' At one point during the concert he moved near her so that they could talk, and one of the things that stood out about her were her odd opinions about the music that was being played. It seemed to Raffaele that she had not been concentrating on the emotions that the music evoked, but rather on its rhythm – 'slow, fast, slow.'

He told his father that during the time that they were together, Amanda had been elusive and Raffaele had thought that 'she was out of this world'. She seemed to live her life like a dream, he said, and seemed detached from reality, as if she was unable to distinguish dreams from what was actually happening. Amanda's life 'seemed to be pure pleasure,' as if she had a 'contact with reality that was almost nonexistent.'

'In the middle of this sad and depressing world,' Raffaele wrote, 'through the window on the other side of the watchtower, on the horizon I can see a small house. And that house on the plain brings out in me a bashful smile of hope.

'I don't know if it's fair that I have to pay such a high price for not paying more attention to the seconds and minutes of November 1. But after this experience, believe me, Dad, I will never smoke another joint in my life. I can now say that I know what it means to take a walk in Hell. And I pray to God not to leave me alone any more. I wait with faith for the results of the investigation which, I know for certain being innocent, will demonstrate what really happened: that I was not in that room when poor Meredith was killed.

'Poor Meredith. A quiet girl who exchanged few words with people, who I had little to do with, but who certainly did not deserve the end she met. I hope that her parents will soon have justice, to know why and how and by whose hand their daughter was killed.'

Raffaele went on to explain how the experience had opened his eyes. He pointed out how he was accustomed to living in a house that was always clean, and that the central heating was on when it was cold.

He wrote of his warm bed, his dream car, and of 'eating the best of the best that the earth has to offer,' and of 'having the best computer on the market and a family that loves me.'

'Here in prison there are people who have none of that,' his letter continued. 'There is a filthy sponge bed, a tiny bathroom with hot water, central heating that is only on for a few hours a day, two quilts and a 13-inch TV. Even the smallest thing in prison can appear precious.'

He explained how he found it all difficult to take in, but that he would be trying to repay everything that he had been given in life. Although he said that he realized that was not enough, he expressed the need to work hard to do something for others as well as for himself.

'I think the key is to love and to love yourself,' he wrote. 'Because everything we have is not anyone's just by right. This experience has at least taught me that.'

Raffaele went on to say that he passed his time in jail by speaking to doctors, psychologists, teachers, guards – anyone that he could engage in conversation – in an attempt to understand 'what could possibly have happened that night in the absolute certainty that I did nothing wrong.'

He said that he tried to understand what Amanda's role was in the terrible ordeal.

'The Amanda I know is an Amanda who lives a

carefree life,' his letter continued. 'Her only thought is the pursuit of pleasure at all times. But even the thought that she could be a killer is impossible for me. I have read her version of events. Some of the things she said are not true, but I don't know why she said them. For example, it wasn't that night that we were in the shower together.

'I can accept that part of the reason we all ended up in prison is my lack of clarity with regards to the events that night. I am paying the price for my own superficiality, and I want to say that I will keep paying down to the last cent. The reality is that my life has changed forever and there is no way back. All I can do is collect the broken pieces and try to put them back together.'

Raffaele's letter was released in its entirety to the Italian press, and detectives combed it, along with Amanda's statements, to try to read between the lines and see if they could discern or eke out anything additional that they could use. Meanwhile, they learned that the results of DNA tests had, in fact, shown that their latest suspect, Rudy Guede, had engaged in sexual contact with Meredith prior to her death. The forensic results were based on a DNA sample taken from a toothbrush at Guede's sleeping room in Perugia and compared with evidence retrieved from Meredith's body. One of his attorneys, Vittorio Lombardo, was quick to point out that the test results did not necessarily mean that Guede was guilty of the murder.

'Rudy has not denied being in Meredith's house, and the tests do not say that the sex was not consensual,' Lombardo said. 'Rudy maintains he was in the bathroom when Meredith was killed, and these tests do not show anything which contradicts that.'

When Guede had appeared before a judge in Koblenz to establish his identity, he told of how he had gone with Meredith to her house. He said he had developed a stomach ache that required him to go to the bathroom and that it was while he was in the bathroom that he had heard Meredith scream. He further stated that Meredith had been killed by 'an Italian guy I don't know,' who fled the residence. He reportedly said that Meredith had whispered the initials 'AF' to him as she expired. He said that he had attempted to save Meredith, but gave in to fear and panic and ran away.

'I took Meredith in my arms,' Guede reportedly told the judge. 'I tried to resuscitate her, but then I panicked and I ran away.'

Lombardo, upon hearing of Guede's statements to the German judge, said that they were given without the presence of legal representation and as such carried no weight in a court of law.

By now, Perugia investigators were also aware of another finding from Edgardo Giobbi of Rome's Serious Crime Squad. Apparently Giobbi had determined that a fingerprint found on the *inside* of Meredith's door matched Raffaele's, despite the fact that he had insisted that he had not gone into her room prior to when he followed police inside on the day her body was discovered. Also troubling was the footprint in blood found inside her room – it matched the size 42 Nike trainers Raffaele owned.

'Rudy Guede wears size 45,' Giobbi said.

However, Giovanni Arcudi, an expert for the defence who planned to argue for Raffaele's release in the coming days, countered with: 'That footprint does not possess clear and definite characteristics.'

On Saturday, November 24, additional CCTV footage damaging to the defence somehow made its way into the media. This time the photos showed Amanda and Raffaele laughing and kissing the day after Meredith's body was found. The latest photos were from the store where Amanda had shopped for lingerie and they had been overheard discussing having 'wild sex' with each other. One of the photos depicted them in a kissing embrace in which they were in full view of other shoppers – shortly after detailing to the police and others how distraught they were over Meredith's murder only a day earlier. Along with the photos came the additional comments from the shopkeeper.

According to Bubbles shopkeeper Carlo Maria Scotto di Rinaldi, Amanda and Raffaele had come into the store on November 3 and were there for about 20 minutes. He recognized them from having seen them on television news programmes.

'The girl bought a camisole and G-string,' di Rinaldi said.

He repeated what he had said earlier, that he had heard them discussing going home to have 'wild sex' as they were getting ready to pay. He said some of the other customers had considered their behaviour in the store 'exhibitionistic'.

'Their behaviour struck me as very odd,' di Rinaldi continued. 'They were laughing and joking as they were holding up the underwear and the girl kept saying she was going to wear it before they had sex. When I realized it was them, and the fact that the poor girl had only been found the day before, their behaviour struck me even more as unusual.'

Meanwhile, soon after learning about Guede's arrest in Germany, Raffaele asked through his attorneys if he could provide new evidence to the prosecutor.

'The situation has changed, and the investigation, now that Rudy Guede has emerged, has changed a great deal,' said one of Raffaele's lawyers, Marco Brusco. 'Our client wants to clarify certain things, but I cannot tell you what they are.'

CHAPTER 13

It was not long after his release from jail that Patrick Lumumba decided to talk publicly about his ordeal regarding the murder of Meredith Kercher. What he had to say seemed to shed light on why he believed an attempt was made to frame him for the crime... and it appeared to lead right back to Amanda Knox.

He told a reporter for *The Mail on Sunday* that he had hired Amanda as a barmaid for Le Chic, his three-storied club that was popular with students for dancing and its specialty rum drinks that they queued eagerly for nightly. Amanda began working – or, rather, showing up for work – at the club about a month before Meredith's death. He thought she would be good for business, and he recalled meeting Amanda and Meredith in late September or early October. He had just opened the club, and one of his friends told him that he knew an American girl who needed a job.

As a result he asked Amanda, through his friend, to come into the bar so they could meet and talk about working there (a seemingly harmless and innocent event, but it set the wheels of fate in motion). She, of course, agreed.

When she showed up, she was dressed in 'flimsy trousers' and was 'full of bravado'. He knew almost immediately that she was exactly the sort of person he wanted to hire.

'She was open and bubbly, and said she'd bring in more customers because she knew everyone,' Lumumba said of that first meeting. 'I didn't find her attractive, but she was confident about the way she looked. It was almost as if she didn't need to wear revealing clothes – she thought she was sexy enough as she was.'

It was that same evening that Amanda introduced Meredith to Patrick. 'Meredith was a natural charmer, a beautiful girl who made friends easily, and received attention wherever she went,' Lumumba said.

He explained that Meredith's Italian was not very good, but she had no problem communicating – many of the residents spoke English anyway and, once comfortable with you, did not mind speaking in English. He told of how she had pointed out an alternative way to make a *mojito*.

'She smiled and commented on the special make of vodka I kept behind the bar,' he explained. 'She said she'd used it herself instead of rum when she was a barmaid making *mojitos* back in Britain.'

He noted that her skin seemed unusually dark to be English, and she told him about her Indian ancestry on her mother's side of the family. When he observed Amanda, Meredith, and the group of girls they were hanging out with that night, Lumumba recalled thinking how close-knit all of them seemed. It had been Latin and Reggae Night at Le Chic, and the girls danced and caught the attention of a number of young men. The next day he told Amanda that she was hired, and that it would be her job, at least at first, to pick up empty or spent glasses at the tables. In his mind it had been a trial arrangement in which she would work two shifts a week, from 10 p.m. to 3 a.m.

Soon after starting the job, Lumumba noticed that Amanda was always flirting with the men who came into the bar, and before long he felt that she had taken the job to 'hit' on the male customers, not to perform actual work. He said that she would regularly place her mouth close enough to the mouths of the men she was talking to that it sometimes looked like they were kissing. She also frequently came in to work late and would just as frequently ask to leave early.

'I'd tell her off, she'd smile sweetly and apologize and be back at it within five minutes,' he said. 'Sometimes when I tried to get her back to work, the men would become rowdy. Someone once told me to mind my own business and "butt out of Amanda's".'

Realizing that Amanda had brought significant business into the bar, he also had the foresight to know that if he did let her go, much of the new business would probably fall off, too, due to negative word-of-mouth publicity. As a result, he decided to tolerate Amanda – for awhile.

Amanda had been employed at the bar for a couple of weeks before Lumumba met Raffaele Sollecito. He came in one evening with a couple of friends, and they began drinking rum and pear juice. After they'd had a few rounds, Lumumba said he observed Amanda flirting with Raffaele in her usual manner. Knowing that Amanda had a boyfriend back home in the U.S., Lumumba had thought at first that all the flirting had been harmless. It was not until he had learned that Amanda and Raffaele had begun dating that Lumumba realized she was two-timing her American boyfriend.

As time went on, Amanda became even lazier when she was supposed to be doing her job at Le Chic. Quite often, when the dance floor was packed and patrons were lining up to get drinks, Amanda was occupied flirting with any man who would give her the time of day – especially those that she liked and found good-looking. During those moments, which comprised the majority of the time supposedly working at the bar, Amanda seemed either unaware that she had work to do or that she could not care less. She must have reasoned that her presence was bringing a good deal of the business into the bar anyway. It had been during one of those moments, around midnight one evening when business was very brisk and about a week before Meredith's death, that Lumumba had decided that he'd had enough of Amanda Knox and decided to fire her.

'She was angry and wanted revenge,' Lumumba said. 'By the end, she hated me.'

Despite his belief that Amanda implicated him in Meredith's murder as revenge for him firing her, Lumumba does not believe that she was evil. He said that a person has to have a soul to be evil, but that Amanda was soulless.

'She's empty, dead inside,' he said. 'She is the ultimate actress, able to switch her emotions on and off in an instant. I don't believe a word she says. Everything that comes out of her mouth is a lie. But those lies have stained me forever… she tried to play the race card. She thought that by pointing the finger at a black person she'd distract attention from herself. She used me as a scapegoat. I've never had so much as a fine for not paying a bus ticket before. But now I've been branded a cold-blooded murderer.'

He went on to describe how charming Meredith was, amiable without even trying. On the other hand, Amanda tried to be charming, too, but ended up being less popular than Meredith. Although he had not realized it at the time, in retrospect he believed that Amanda had been jealous of Meredith.

'She always wanted to be the queen bee,' Lumumba said. 'As the weeks passed, it became clear that she wasn't. She hated anyone stealing her limelight, including Meredith.'

Sometime in October, perhaps towards the middle of the month and about a week before he had fired Amanda, Lumumba threw a party at the bar for the staff. He said that Meredith had shown up, and she made her special vodka *mojitos* for everyone, which they enjoyed. He described her as 'sparkly and cheery' and said that she had 'lifted everyone's spirits.' He said he had met Meredith by chance in town soon after the party, and he asked her if she would like to work behind the bar the next time he had a DJ, on a ladies' night.

'She jumped at the chance,' he said, 'although she had stopped coming into Le Chic. And I heard that she wasn't hanging around with Amanda much, either. I wasn't surprised. The two couldn't have been more different.'

By then, he said, Amanda had become more erratic and even more unreliable, if that was possible. Her mood swings became more obvious as they changed from simply being 'docile and lazy to hyperactive and flighty'. He said that he knew she was smoking pot, and it soon became impossible to foresee which mood she would be in on any given day. He said that he had told her that he had asked Meredith to come and work for him at the bar.

'Her face dropped and there was a big silence,' he said. 'Then she said, "Fine," and stormed off. I knew then that she was extremely jealous of Meredith. She obviously thought Meredith was invading her territory.'

After reflecting a bit, Lumumba said that the situation between him and Amanda had come to a head on Tuesday, October 30, the day he recalled as having fired her. When he told her that he could no longer use her in the bar but said that she could continue handing out flyers for Le Chic, she looked at him impassively and walked away. He said that he did not see her again that evening.

Lumumba recalled that she returned to the bar the following night, Halloween, to attend the party being held there. She drank a lot of free red wine, and 'was all over two American boys.' Lumumba said he had not seen Raffaele at the party that evening, and he had not noticed when Amanda left. He said he locked up Le Chic at 3 a.m. and went to another club where he encountered Meredith.

'I mentioned the idea of her working for me again,' he said. 'She smiled sweetly and said she couldn't wait, and she'd bring all her friends back to the club for me.'

Lumumba said that had been the last time that he had seen Meredith.

The next time he heard anything about Meredith had been at approximately 6 p.m. on Saturday, November 3, when two of his friends came into the bar and asked him if he had heard that 'Amanda's English friend had been murdered.' When he looked at them quizzically, as if to ask them who they were referring to, his friends told him that they were talking about 'the dark-skinned girl'.

'My heart stopped,' Lumumba said.

He called Amanda, who confirmed that Meredith was indeed dead and that she had been murdered. He said that he had expected Amanda to be 'distraught, hysterical and sobbing,' but she was not. Instead, he said she had sounded 'weird,' the tone of her voice 'completely flat.' She had seemed 'calm and unaffected' as well, not at all the way one would expect someone whose roommate had been murdered to be.

'She said she was talking to the police and hung up,' Lumumba said. 'I was shaken and sick with sadness. Things like this just didn't happen in Perugia.'

CHAPTER 14

More than two weeks after Meredith had been murdered, the majority of Perugia's 162,000 residents were still talking about the horrible affair. It seemed like much of the city had become tense and suspicious of those they came into contact with, and a number of people had become increasingly upset over the treatment Lumumba had received from the police. In fact, after he had told his story to *The Mail on Sunday*, the story of how his arrest had come about was on the minds of many people and it had become one of the most talked about aspects of the case over drinks in Perugia's many bars.

The story was told best, of course, by Lumumba himself. He was at home in his fourth-floor flat with his girlfriend and their son at 6.30 a.m. on Tuesday, November 6, when someone began buzzing his doorbell repeatedly. As he walked towards the door, a woman's voice on the other side was demanding that he open it, by order of the police. As soon as he opened the door, the woman, accompanied by as many as 15 to 20 other people, entered. None of them wore uniforms, but they were carrying guns. With no idea why they were at his flat, Lumumba did not at first realise that they were the police, so their presence and actions frightened him and his family.

Lumumba was handcuffed and whisked outside to one of seven police cars and was swiftly driven to police headquarters where he was placed inside an interrogation room.

Making matters worse, Lumumba did not even know at that point what it was that he was supposed to have done. Frightened and humiliated like he had never been before, about two hours into what turned into a 10-hour interrogation one of the inquisitors suggested that one of his colleagues show him a photo of 'the dead girl' in an attempt to get him 'to confess'.

'It might sound naïve,' he said, 'but it was only then that I made the connection between Meredith's death and my arrest. Stunned, I said, "You think I killed Meredith?"'

Lumumba's questioners finally showed him the evidence they had against him. By then it was about 5.30 p.m., and the bulk of what they had shown him was Amanda's statement in which she had told the police that he had persuaded her to take him to the cottage she shared with Meredith and how she had accused him of raping Meredith before killing her in her room while Amanda sat in the kitchen. He had difficulty believing that Amanda had told the police that the alleged rape and murder was a result of Lumumba's revenge after Meredith had rejected him.

'It was only then that I realized just how mad she was,' he said. 'I had no sexual feelings towards Meredith, and have never cheated on [my girlfriend]... what Amanda was saying was insane. I have seven sisters and there's no way I could even imagine hurting a woman.'

Despite the fact that he was filled with anger, Lumumba also knew that he needed to remain calm while in the presence of the police, even though he knew that their evidence was flawed and that they could not possibly have any evidence against him that could stand up in court. He knew that once investigators had compared the blood sample and fingerprints taken from him upon his arrival at Capanne prison where he was held, it would be all over and that they would have little choice but to release him.

During the two weeks that the police held him, he watched the details of the case as they unfolded each day on the TV in his cell. He was shocked and appalled by the sordid details of Amanda's and Raffaele's lifestyle.

'That kind of life was foreign to me, and it made me sick that people would think I was involved in some kind of threesome. I knew students slept around, but to hear rumours of sex games with knives shocked me to the core. As far as I am concerned, anyone involved in such things needs psychiatric help.'

Lumumba knew that he had never been to their house, that it 'was a mistake' and that he would eventually be released when the police realized that Amanda had lied about him. After hearing his side of the story about Amanda and Meredith, the police now had to consider Amanda's jealousy of Meredith as a motive, albeit a slim one, for the murder. Although he acknowledged that his reputation had been permanently damaged by the ordeal, Lumumba, being a parent himself, had difficulty imagining what Meredith's parents were going through.

'I hope they get some peace when the killer is caught,' he said. 'I don't always think Amanda did it, but I think she knows who did it, and whoever killed Meredith should stay in prison forever.'

The last time he saw Amanda was outside the university's library, on the Monday after the murder and prior to the arrests. 'Despite all my misgivings of her, I wanted to give her comfort and support,' he said. 'I told her I was so sorry about Meredith. She seemed completely normal. But she had a nasty look in her eyes and simply said I had no idea what it was like to be probed by police for hours on end. Well, thanks to her, I know exactly what she's going through now, and I'll never forgive her.'

Meanwhile, the case fast-forwarded to Wednesday, December 6, 2007, the day Rudy Guede was extradited to Italy. During his initial statements to Italian police, Guede made no mention of Amanda Knox or Raffaele Sollecito, but he did provide what seemed like a highly implausible account of what happened in the cottage the evening Meredith was killed, and insisted that the sex between him and Meredith had been consensual after investigators told him that they had found strands of hair in one of Meredith's hands that forensics experts had matched to him.

According to his version of events that evening, Guede said that he had bumped into Meredith and that she had asked him to her flat for a drink. He said that they had arrived at the cottage at approximately 8.30 p.m. The timeline of his account, however, seemed flawed, as it did not match the timings provided by Meredith's friends, Sophie Purton and Robyn Butterworth, both of whom had watched *The Notebook* with her and said that she had not left Purton's flat until about 9 p.m.

He was now telling the police that when he left Meredith's room that evening to go to the bathroom, he had put on his iPod headphones. Perhaps surprisingly, he had been able to hear Meredith scream, despite wearing the headphones. He repeated his story of having seen an unknown assailant who, he claimed, had entered the cottage and had killed Meredith.

'He was an Italian lad with chestnut hair,' Guede said. 'We knocked into each other. I was also injured, but I cannot remember clearly the face of that man. Then I ran away. I was scared. I am not the one who killed her.'

He said that he had decided to flee Italy because he was afraid that he would be blamed for the murder which, he said, he did not commit. The police, however, challenged his account and said that forensic examination had shown that Meredith had not engaged in 'consensual sex' as Guede had claimed, but had most likely been held down during sex.

Before fleeing, however, he said he went home and changed clothes, and then went to the Domus disco where he danced and drank from about 2 a.m. until 4.30 a.m. on Friday, November 2. Although it was, of course, possible the events had occurred just as Guede had said, it just did not seem likely at that point. It also did not seem feasible that a person who had witnessed a supposed killer fleeing the scene of a crime would go out dancing and drinking – especially after holding a dying young woman in his arms before leaving.

According to the police, the picture of Guede that was emerging was one of a misfit who had an obsession for foreign girls. He was known to hang out in Perugia's main square, where young people – including students –were known to smoke cannabis and drink late at night. Guede had been involved in a stabbing at the square earlier in the year. By the time of their interviews with Guede, investigators believed more firmly than ever that Meredith had been murdered during or after a party in which sex and drugs had been involved. The chief prosecutor, Giuliano Mignini, however, even though he strongly felt that there was a connection between Amanda, Raffaele and Guede, expressed doubts that the three suspects would make a concerted effort to protect each other. Nonetheless, Mignini pushed forward with his theory that all three had been at the scene of the murder that night and had even taken part in it.

To help reinforce Mignini's theory, Judge Maurizio Bufali later wrote that the evidence to date strongly indicated that 'a group participation in the heinous crime in which a passive role does not appear plausible for any of those present.'

Mignini, meanwhile, made it clear that he did not believe Guede's version of what had occurred that evening, calling it a 'rather improbable account'. Mignini repeated that the door to Meredith's house had not been forced open and therefore had not shown signs of a break-in despite Guede's claims that an 'unknown Italian' had killed Meredith. He also pointed out how the house had been cleaned up by someone after the murder.

As Guede was growing up, his adopted family sent him to the Vittorio Emanuele II school, one of the finest schools in Perugia. However, it appeared that he had not taken his studies seriously and he eventually became involved in drugs and his character quickly took a turn for the worse.

'I was trying to help Rudy build a future,' Paolo Caporali said. 'I thought I gave him a good opportunity. But he revealed himself to be a great liar. He would say he would go to lessons, and then skip them. His results were lousy.'

Caporali said that Guede preferred sitting in front of the TV, playing video games, to studying or going to school. He had little or no interest in work, either. 'When I realized what was happening, I wanted to distance him from my family,' Caporali said. 'He went away.'

Caporali added that Guede eventually returned to Perugia, in January 2007, at which time Caporali offered him a second chance by helping him find work as a gardener. Caporali conceded that his efforts to help Guede had been another mistake when Guede disappeared again in August. He said the next time he heard anything about Rudy Guede was when detectives investigating Meredith's murder knocked on his door.

Meanwhile, back in the UK, three weeks after the murder Meredith Kercher's parents had been left in limbo over arranging a funeral and burying their daughter, despite the fact that her body had been flown home. The Italian authorities opposed a burial because of a request by attorneys for the defence after Lumumba's legal counsel had initially asked for a second autopsy in an effort to establish a more precise time of death. The request had more or less become a moot issue after Lumumba's release, but in the interim Raffaele Sollecito's lawyers had also asked for a second autopsy to establish whether the wounds on Meredith's body were compatible with the knife seized at his home. The forensic pathologist, Luca Lalli, who had performed the original postmortem examination, told a judge who was to decide on whether Meredith's funeral should go ahead or not, that he was adamant that a second autopsy was unnecessary because everything done during the original examination had been recorded.

The good news was that a judge had sided with Lalli in the decision to allow burial, bringing a certain amount of relief for Meredith's grieving family.

'It's good news, very good news, and gives the family a tiny bit of closure,' Meredith's mother, Arline Kercher, said after hearing of the decision. 'However, this is far from over. There is still a long way to go. Our family will not be able to rest fully until the person or people who killed Meredith are locked up in prison. This is some small consolation but ultimately we want justice for Meredith.'

She said that their family could still not believe that Meredith was gone. 'It's still raw and extremely shocking for us,' she continued. 'The last few weeks have been like a nightmare. It has been devastating, and tragic. At least now we might be able to start planning her funeral... and hopefully now she will be laid to rest and have peace... I want to see her killers punished for what they have done. They have torn our family apart. Meredith has been taken away from us forever. We will never be able to have peace.'

CHAPTER 15

As the investigation into Meredith's murder continued, detectives began to theorize that robbery may have been a motive. Although it had been quickly discounted during the early days of the investigation, the police were revisiting the idea when they learned that Meredith had withdrawn 250 euros from her bank two days before she was killed. The money, detectives believed, was to pay her rent. Her landlord, however, said that the rent money had not been received.

The robbery motive theory was given at least some credence when Rudy Guede told the investigators that when he arrived at the cottage with Meredith, she had gone into her room and opened a drawer and noticed that cash, presumably part of which had been her rent money, was missing. He claimed that she then went into Amanda's room to see if the money was there, at the same time complaining that Amanda was always 'doing drugs' and that she was fed up with her. Upon hearing Guede's story, the police speculated that Amanda may have stolen the money from Meredith to buy drugs – possibly from Guede. In that scenario police theorized that either the missing money or Meredith expressing her dissatisfaction to Amanda about her use of drugs, or both, may have led to a confrontation between the two that had also led to Meredith's death.

On hearing the speculation, Amanda's family dismissed it as 'ridiculous' – even more so than the earlier sex attack theory. To support their argument, the family said that Amanda had no need to steal any money from Meredith because she had thousands of dollars of her own money in her bank account – money she had saved from a number of jobs and from donations by family members who had helped her out with her college fund. Similarly, Raffaele came from a wealthy family, drove an expensive car, and had no reason to become involved in stealing money. Guede, a number of people pointed out, was the one person out of the trio who did need money, and some even suggested that he had implicated Amanda at the encouragement of the police.

Investigator Edgardo Giobbi, a member of the Rome Serious Crimes Squad, equivalent to the FBI in the U.S., had his own theories about the missing money. According to Giobbi, police examined Meredith's cash machine withdrawals prior to her death and found that most had been for about 30 euros at a time – except for the withdrawal of the 250 euros two days before her death. Despite the protestations from Amanda's family, Giobbi supported the theory that Meredith may have accused Amanda of stealing from her.

'That accusation, which Kercher possibly made in front of Rudy Guede, sparked a row,' proposed Giobbi. 'Kercher… withdrew around… 250 euros two days before her death, most likely to pay her rent. Her landlord did not receive the money, and there is no trace of it, although Amanda Knox was carrying 215 euros when she was taken into custody.'

Of course, there was no proof that she had stolen money from Meredith – only the *possibility* that she had done so. The 215 euros in Amanda's possession could just as easily have been her own money. It was also possible, Giobbi continued, that Amanda and Guede were alone together at the cottage when Meredith came home at around 9 p.m.

'Alternatively, Guede may have stolen the money from Kercher's room which he then used to pay for his train ticket to Germany,' Giobbi added.

Meanwhile, the Italian police said that yet another crucial piece of evidence had surfaced. A bloody fingerprint, they said, was found on a water tap in the bathroom next to Meredith's room. Giuliano Mignini said it belonged to Amanda Knox and suggested that she could have been cut in a violent struggle.

Mignini's many critics however – including experts hired by the defence legal teams – argued that the fingerprint could have come about in any number of ways. It was possible, they said, that she had injured herself in a manner that had absolutely nothing to do with the crime. After all, she had lived in the same flat as Meredith and two other girls, and the fingerprint could have been the result of a simple domestic accident.

At a hearing for her release, experts also argued that the knife bearing Meredith's DNA and Amanda's DNA near the handle was inconclusive. Experts would be willing to testify in court that the knife in question could not have been used to inflict two out of the three slash wounds to Meredith's neck. The knife also did not match an imprint left in blood on a bed sheet at the crime scene. Amanda's DNA could have been on the knife because she had probably used it in the preparation of food at Raffaele's flat. Meredith's DNA, although a match, had been at such a low level that it would be discarded in courts of law in the U.S. and Britain, and defence experts said that it could have got onto the knife through cross-contamination from other DNA in the laboratory. Because of the large amount of blood at the crime scene, the knife – if it was the murder weapon – should have had equally large amounts of Meredith's DNA on it.

After hearing Mignini argue that the three suspects might flee Italy if freed, the judges decided that the suspects should remain in jail while investigation continued. Amanda responded to this in a somewhat positive manner by saying that 'when all this is finished, here is where I want to live.' While it was generally believed that by this she meant Perugia and not Capanne prison, she did characterize her prison cellmates as 'marvellous', adding, 'and the other prisoners are also very nice with me. We have spent time together. We do a load of things together.'

Now that she was being housed with prisoners convicted of crimes similar to those she was suspected of committing, including murderers and sex offenders, Amanda appeared more peaceful and composed than when she first arrived.

'The first few days I spent in isolation,' she told a reporter for *Corriere Della Sera*. 'It was very hard. I couldn't have any relations with anyone... my God, those days were terrible. Nobody said a word to me. I thought I was going mad and I prayed that they would move me. When I arrived here, everything changed. They treat me with great dignity. It's important.'

Before the year was over it was revealed that authorities at Capanne prison had confiscated Amanda's diary and again, like previous documents and information, sections of it were leaked to the press. Some entries showed that Amanda had changed her story about the night of Meredith's murder once again. This time she had claimed that Raffaele had framed her for the crime – one in which she said he committed after playing a violent sex game. It seemed somewhat ironic that the details of her latest claim were made public shortly after she had apologized to Lumumba for falsely accusing him.

'That night I smoked a lot of marijuana and I fell asleep at my boyfriend's house,' read an excerpt from the 50-page diary. 'I don't remember anything. But I think it's possible that Raffaele went to Meredith's house, raped her, then killed her, and then when he got home, while I was sleeping, he put my fingerprints on the knife. But I can't begin to understand why Raffaele would do that.'

Certain diary entries appeared to contradict taped conversations between Amanda and her parents, surreptitiously obtained, during visits at the prison. In one of those conversations Amanda had said: 'It's stupid. I can't say anything else. I was there [at the flat]. I can't say anything else, there is no reason to.'

In her diary, however, she wrote that if she had been with Meredith the night she was killed, Meredith 'would still be alive'. Why the contradictions? Was she simply trying to divert attention from herself?

In other parts of her diary Amanda's vanity became apparent. In one entry she wrote that when she got an hour of 'outside time', she sat with her face towards the sun to get a tan. Prisoners at Capanne are allowed one hour outside during every 24-hour period.

'I have received letters from fellow inmates and

admirers telling me that I am hot and they want to have sex with me,' read another entry. 'I have also had insulting letters.' Another entry, described as chilling, recounted that she had travelled through Europe with a 'kitchen knife in my bag'.

Six weeks after her murder, on Friday, December 14, 2007, Meredith's family finally laid her body to rest at a private service for family and friends at a church near her home in South London. Dozens of Meredith's friends from the University of Leeds, where she studied prior to going to Perugia, as well as other local friends, attended the service. Meredith's family followed the casket, adorned with colourful flowers and her photograph, into the church. One of the floral decorations spelt out her nickname, 'Mez', with small yellow flowers. There were a number of tribute floral arrangements, including one that read, 'You will always be in our hearts'. Another small bouquet was 'From the City of Perugia', and a card attached to a bouquet of white roses read, 'Why such a tragic waste? May your smile be infectious in Heaven, Mez.' Two large pillow-shaped arrangements made from small blue flowers were placed outside, one on either side of the church entrance. The funeral was followed by a private burial at the nearby Mitcham Road Cemetery.

Chapter 16

On Saturday, December 22, 2007, police investigators revealed that Amanda had given herself away when she purportedly provided details of Meredith's murder to friends and acquaintances – details, police insist, that would be known only to the killer and to the police. One of the facts that she had allegedly revealed was that Meredith had died slowly from a stab wound to the neck. Another, which had been provided to the police by Robyn Butterworth, was that Amanda said that she had seen Meredith's body reflected in the mirror of the wardrobe in her room.

'The question is,' asked a source for the prosecution, 'how did she know these particular details, as only police and the killer would have been aware of them?'

The information, as much of it had been from day one, was revealed in the media, this time in an article by Nick Piza, a reporter for the *Daily Mail*. The headline for Piza's article had screamed out like the title of a story from an old issue of *True Detective* magazine: 'Foxy Knoxy and the clue "only a killer would know"'. That headline, and countless others like it, had only touched the surface of what really happened, as was evident by information revealed when the *MSNBC* news agency sent former FBI profiler Clint Van Zandt to Perugia. A one-time supervisor in the FBI's Behavioral Science Unit, Van Zandt was now an analyst for NBC News and his job in this assignment was to help interpret the crime scene evidence and how Meredith had died. In particular, his report described just how gruesome and painful a death Meredith's killers had put her through.

Van Zandt's information was made possible by the chief investigators in Italy's national crime lab, who gave him and NBC News access to Meredith's murder file, a practice almost unheard of in the U.S. and the UK until after a case has been adjudicated. Every country has its own rules, regulations and standards that it follows, and it was thought that the decision to make the file accessible had the potential to assist police in the investigation rather than hindering them.

At any rate, information and photos in the file indicated that a large-bladed knife had entered the left side of the victim's neck and come out the other side. A common kitchen knife such as that taken from Raffaele's apartment fitted the bill which, according to the file, investigators believe may have been the murder weapon. Although analysts contended that the knife had been scrubbed with bleach, DNA traces belonging to both Amanda and Meredith were pointed out to Van Zandt.

Van Zandt also saw photos depicting a large quantity of blood on Meredith's hands. This suggested, he deduced, that she had reached up and grabbed her throat with her hands after she had realized that a knife had just been put through her neck. Bleeding profusely from the wound, she would have also reached backwards in an effort to hold herself up or push herself up, Van Zandt said. He also believed that the location of the foreign DNA on her body and the location and trajectory of the blood spray from her wound supported the investigators' theory that Meredith was being sexually attacked from behind when she was killed. It was possible that she was bent over, or that someone was forcing her to her knees and threatening her with the knife before actually plunging it through her neck.

Van Zandt took his theory a step further, saying that whoever killed Meredith had most likely threatened her with a knife first, to get her attention and to tell her that she was going to comply with whatever it was they wanted to do to her.

At some point, for whatever reason, after taunting her with the knife and causing the minor superficial wounds, something happened that caused the person wielding the knife to decide to kill her. Perhaps she had threatened her attackers during the sexual part of the assault by telling them that she was going to turn them into the police, and she was killed to prevent that from happening. Or perhaps the killer just wanted the thrill of knowing what it felt like to kill someone. Whatever the reason, after the knife had been plunged all the way through her neck, Meredith died from drowning in her own blood.

After surveying the crime scene, Van Zandt expressed the opinion that it was highly unlikely that an intruder had broken into the cottage, as the suspects had claimed, primarily because the broken window was situated some 15 feet above a steep slope. To the former criminal profiler, it just did not seem like a plausible way into the cottage, and he sided with the Italian investigators who believed that the break-in had been staged. All-in-all, he believed the investigators had done a good job piecing the case together with evidence that led back to Amanda, Raffaele, and now, Rudy Guede.

Meanwhile, Italian police revealed additional information about their interview with Rudy Guede following his return from Germany. In addition to saying that he had been inside the cottage on the night of the murder and had consensual sex with Meredith – sticking by his story that someone had broken in and killed her while he was in the bathroom – he had purportedly told the detectives that he thought the brown-haired Italian male he had seen when he came out of the bathroom may have been Raffaele, who he claimed he did not know well. Whoever the man was, Guede told the police that the intruder had insulted him with a racial slur in Italian before leaving. He also claimed that he had heard Amanda's voice, but that he had not seen her. He told the police that he had only met her once, at Le Chic, but nonetheless suggested that perhaps Amanda had mistaken him for Patrick Lumumba that night. The detectives were reluctant to buy into the suggestion, however, because the age difference between Rudy Guede and Lumumba is more than 20 years. Besides, aside from the colour of their skin they bore little resemblance to one another.

Police sources further stated that Guede's DNA had been found on Meredith's bra, which detectives now say was 'ripped off' her body during the attack. Combined with his statements to the police and others, not to mention the physical evidence that had been recovered, there was no doubt that Guede had been at the crime scene.

'His version of events is full of lies and contradictions,' Mignini said. 'His DNA is on the victim and on the bra.'

On Friday, January 11, 2008, it was revealed that Italian forensic teams working over the Christmas and New Year's holidays had isolated DNA from Raffaele Sollecito on a bra hook that had been found in

December attached to another fragment of material that was not disclosed, following an additional search of Meredith's room. Apparently the bra hook had been overlooked during initial searches of the crime scene, but the new evidence was enough to convince detectives that all three had been 'actively involved' in Meredith's murder.

'The fact that Sollecito's DNA was found on the bra puts him at the crime scene,' said a police source, while Raffaele, through his lawyer, Marco Brusco, had expressed 'surprise' that his DNA was found on the bra.

'As I have already said,' Brusco added, 'we shall await the full report before saying anything, but my client is surprised to hear his DNA has been found.'

Hours later, investigators announced that they had used the chemical Luminol to look for traces of blood inside the house where Meredith was killed, and had found a bare footprint left in blood in Amanda's bedroom.

When sprayed on surfaces at a crime scene, Luminol will detect blood, even when it has been cleaned up. A chemical reaction to iron in blood causes the chemical to 'glow' when used at night or under artificial black lighting, usually lasting about 30 seconds, long enough for investigators to photograph or otherwise document its presence.

'This is a crucial discovery and very important,' said Edgardo Giobbi. 'It was discovered during the examination of the apartment and was in Amanda's bedroom. At this stage we do not know if it was made by a man or a woman. It will be compared to the three suspects. There were also traces of blood found between the room and other parts of the apartment. Luminol also showed up traces of blood in Meredith's bathroom and these are also being investigated.'

On Thursday, January 24, just when it had begun to look like the twists and turns of this bizarre case were subsiding, news was released that an Albanian man had come forward and told police and prosecutors that Amanda Knox had threatened him with a knife the day before Meredith's body was found. In his statement, the Albanian said that while he was parking his car near the house where the murder occurred he bumped into a waste container. Two people came out from behind the container, and an argument ensued.

'On the evening of 31st October I arrived in my car close to the house on Via della Pergola,' the Albanian witness said. 'As I was parking my car I hit a rubbish dumpster. A second later I saw two people, a man and a woman, who were behind it and they came towards me, shouting. We started arguing and then all of a sudden the girl pulled out a knife. She was shouting at me and pointing it at me. I am certain it was Amanda Knox, and with her was Raffaele Sollecito. Then, out of the darkness emerged another man. It was Rudy. The three of them were together... I've only come forward now because I was scared. I spoke with a lawyer before coming to see you but in the end I realized it was important.'

When this latest bombshell was made public, the police eventually admitted that they had known about the man's purported encounter with the three suspects for some time, but said that the information had been kept secret because of its importance to the integrity of the case. The revelation, however, prompted a response from Mignini.

'This is a very serious matter,' Mignini said. 'This statement was a secret and now it is in the public domain. I am not prepared to say anything else about it.'

The fact that Mignini even acknowledged the existence of the Albanian's statement suggested its importance to the prosecution's case and helped to further establish that the three murder suspects knew each other. Unidentified police sources also said that the man's statement had been checked, including details such as that it had been raining that night, and there were other verifiable portions, such as when garbage containers are set out for pick-up and the locations where they are placed, among other details, had been shown to be correct.

'He is an Albanian with a regular resident's permit and he has no criminal record,' said an unidentified source close to the investigation. 'His story is being taken seriously as it proves that all three suspects knew each other. Knox and Sollecito have both denied knowing Rudy but this man's statement puts them together and with a knife 24 hours before poor Meredith was murdered. It also suggests that the three were out there, armed with a knife and already planning this murder when they were disturbed and it [the murder] was put back a day. He is being taken as a serious and credible witness.'

By this point in the investigation – in part because of Rudy Guede's 'Vampire' YouTube video in which he said, 'I drink blood' – detectives were beginning to examine a theory that Meredith had been murdered as part of a black magic ritual. It was suggested that the theory was being explored because of the prosecutor's enthusiasm regarding conspiracy theories, and the fact that Mignini had long been fascinated, as is much of the public in Italy, with cases involving black magic and satanic worship.

'This suggestion is being looked at primarily because of the date that the murder took place, November 1, which is All Saints Day, and the following day is All Soul's Day, also known as the Day of the Dead,' said a police source.

All Soul's Day is a Roman Catholic day of remembrance for friends and loved ones who have died, and originates from the ancient pagans who celebrated a 'Festival of the Dead', in which it was thought that the souls of the deceased return for a meal with the family they left behind. Candles are placed in windows, believed to help guide the souls back to their home. All Soul's Day follows All Saints Day as a reminder to Catholics that the faithful need to alter their focus from the souls in heaven to the souls in purgatory.

It is said that satanic worship has become somewhat widespread in Italy and at other locations across the Continent over the past several years. Contributing to the theory that Meredith's murder may have been part of a satanic or black magic ritual was the fact that her throat had been slashed, resulting in much blood at the murder scene, and the fact that her body was partially nude when she was killed. Sexual abuse, including rape, is another characteristic sometimes found in such rituals.

By the end of January 2008 it was said that investigators had also found traces of DNA on Meredith's bra that did not match any of the three suspects. This suggested that other people, besides the three suspects, may have been involved in her death, or that she'd had some kind of contact with at least one other person. It was also possible that the additional DNA was the result of cross-contamination, perhaps in the crime laboratory.

Meanwhile, a group calling itself 'Friends of Amanda' was set up and began acting as a sort of advocate for Amanda in the press, both in the U.S. and abroad. A Chicago criminal investigator was involved, working on the case for free, as was Seattle attorney Anne Bremner.

It was pointed out that the group did not represent Amanda Knox or her family in any official capacity. It appeared that the group merely acted as a watchdog, concerned primarily with how Amanda was being portrayed in the media.

By Friday, February 1, it was revealed publicly that DNA belonging to Rudy Guede had been found on Meredith's bloody handbag. It was said that investigators believed the DNA had come from Guede's sweat. Traces of blood were also found inside the handbag, adding further credence to a police theory that Meredith's murder may have been motivated by theft of money and credit cards. Police had also announced that they were trying to locate two of Meredith's credit cards that were unaccounted for.

'The DNA was a match for Guede's and there was also Meredith's blood inside the handbag,' said a police source. 'Checks are still being carried out to see if there is any DNA from others inside the handbag. The theory we are working on is that the killer rifled through Meredith's handbag and took her rent money.'

'We have been informed about this but our position has not changed,' said Guede's lawyer, Vittorio Lombardo. 'We have always said that Guede was at the house that night and he has admitted it himself. It is clear that the police will find his DNA there, on the bag and elsewhere. But it does not mean he is the killer.'

Also, Luca Lalli, the pathologist who performed the

autopsy on Meredith's body, also said it was possible that the 'sexual violence Meredith suffered may have been simulated to make it look as if she had been the victim of a sex attack.' The DNA found on Meredith's body that had been matched to Guede had come from 'finger skin cells and not sperm,' Lalli had concluded. Lalli also said that he believed the sex attack had been faked because he had not found any 'bruising consistent with a rape' on Meredith's body. It was now being said in a new report that 'there are elements which suggest Meredith was involved in recent sexual activity before she died, but from the data obtained it is impossible to say whether it was consensual or not.'

The report raised new questions about the sexual aspect of the case. If Meredith had engaged in sex with someone recently, how recently had it occurred and with whom? Before her boyfriend had left town? He had already told police that they'd had sex. And if not with her boyfriend, then who? However it turned out, the new finding served to diminish – if not eliminate – a sexual motive for Meredith's murder.

CHAPTER 17

On Wednesday, March 26, 2008, investigators moved Rudy Guede from his prison cell to an interrogation room where he underwent intense questioning for nearly six hours about his involvement in the Meredith Kercher murder and what he knew about the involvement of anyone else. His questioners came out of the session seemingly pleased, and said that he had provided a confession that amounted to a 'nail in the coffin' in the case. It was the first time that any of the three suspects had directly blamed each other for the crime to investigators, and although he had again denied having anything to do with the murder he had said that both Amanda and Raffaele had been at the house when Meredith was killed. Investigators had believed all along that, given enough time, one of the suspects would 'break' and reveal what they really knew about that night.

'Amanda and Raffaele were at the house that night,' Guede told investigators. 'I saw them. When I came out of the bathroom I saw a male figure. I put my hand on his shoulder and he had a knife in his hand. I also heard Amanda Knox. She was at the door. I saw her there. The two girls hated each other. It was a row over money that sparked it off. Meredith accused Amanda of stealing 250 euro from her drawer.'

Although Guede had previously mentioned the 'Italian' man he had seen in the cottage the night of the murder, he had never named him. Guede told investigators that he recognized Sollecito from photographs that were shown to him while being questioned.

'All I can say is that we were very pleased with what Guede had to say,' Mignini said after the lengthy interrogation. 'It was very, very useful to the investigation and we will be putting it all in the file which we will present later this spring.'

A source in the prosecutor's office called Guede's statement 'a significant breakthrough,' although Raffaele's lawyers and his family failed to see it as such – understandable considering what it meant for Raffaele.

'This version of events was planned and agreed beforehand,' read a prepared statement from Raffaele's family that was released to the media afterwards. 'What he [Guede] says is totally unfounded and without proof. He is saying all this now after months in jail. It is also interesting to note that it comes less than a week before the application for the removal of custody [hearing]. At the same time it is also interesting to read of the prosecution's satisfaction and that's because it was all agreed and planned beforehand.'

Luca Maori, one of Raffaele's attorneys, said that he would be waiting to 'see the full statement and see exactly what it says' before making any direct comments pertaining to Guede's interview.

'But it strikes me as being an unlikely account and comes from someone who is also very hard to believe,' Maori said. 'It is the act of someone who is in a desperate situation.'

'It is further damning evidence for the case... for the prime suspects,' Valter Biscotti, Guede's attorney, said. 'We were delighted with how it went. Guede again stressed his complete non involvement in the murder.'

Guede's statement came a week before all three suspects were scheduled to appear in front of the Supreme Court in Rome to make an appeal to be freed on bail. None of the suspects had yet been formally charged.

Shortly after Guede's statement, Telenorba, a local television station in Bari, Raffaele's home town, broadcast an official police forensic film that showed the crime scene and graphic footage of Meredith's body. After learning about the airing from their attorney, John and Arline Kercher were, needless to say, 'shocked and distressed' that they and their daughter had been victimized once again. Although the film was part of a documentary about the case, *Perfect Crime or Imperfect Investigation*, intended to show that the investigation into Meredith's murder had not been handled well, the police footage in question was about three minutes long.

'This is an example of gross journalistic misconduct, which evidently violates all the rules of how to report a story,' the Kerchers' attorney, Francesco Maresca, said. 'I spoke with Stephanie Kercher, Meredith's sister, about the programme and she was shocked and upset. At the moment, I do not know whether the family intends to pursue a court case against this pathetic journalistic initiative, but obviously the editor of the programme will have to take responsibility for it... We are looking at the possibility of legal action.'

The Kercher family and their lawyer were not the only people outraged by the broadcast. Italy's Order of Journalists immediately asked that the video be confiscated so that it could not be shown again, and a scheduled rebroadcast was cancelled. The editor of the programme, Enzo Magistra, defended the showing and was adamant that it was not intended to offend anyone.

'When I decided to transmit the images of Meredith's corpse, I did not have the least intention of violating anyone's dignity, but merely to do my job with respect to an important event,' Magistra said.

Unlike in the U.S., it is typically not unusual for

graphic images and film footage about atrocities to be broadcast on Italian television and also throughout much of Europe. Greater freedom regarding censorship seems to be exercised in the region, but many felt that a line had been crossed, an unspoken barrier broken, because of the sensitivity surrounding the Meredith Kercher case.

'For five minutes of television, the ultimate taboo has been broken without any shame,' said Anna Maria Ferretti, director of the Italian TV channel Antenna Sud.

On Tuesday, April 1, the Court of Cassation, Italy's top criminal court, heard arguments for the release from prison of Amanda Knox, Raffaele Sollecito, and Rudy Guede. However, the court rejected their appeals and ordered all three suspects to remain behind bars as the police continued with their investigation.

In early April 2008, Judge Claudia Matteini ordered that three independent experts report on findings in a new postmortem report designed to shed more light on the case. Once again, information about the report was leaked to the press before the scheduled release date. Unlike in the U.S. and Britain, it is not unlawful to release potentially damaging or prejudicial information during an ongoing investigation. A panel of judges typically makes up a jury in criminal cases in Italy, and it is presumed that a judge or other official will not be swayed by what he or she reads in a newspaper or sees on television news shows. As a result, the new report raised the possibility that Meredith may have been killed with two knives instead of one, and that she may have suffocated as opposed to having bled to death as originally believed.

The report also suggested that Meredith may have died during the early hours of the morning and not within the time-frame originally put forward. Unfortunately, because her body temperature was not recorded until approximately 11 hours after her death, the actual time that she died might never be known.

The new report also showed that Meredith's blood alcohol level was nearly three times the legal limit for driving, and said that she was on the 'verge of a drunken stupor' when she was killed. This conflicted with earlier reports in which witnesses had told police that she did not have anything to drink with dinner that evening. Combined with earlier information that a piece of mushroom had been found in her throat, suggesting that perhaps she had eaten pizza at some point that evening, along with her blood alcohol level being what it was, may have been an indication that she had not left Sophie Purton's home at around 9 p.m. as originally believed but had, perhaps, left earlier, and stopped off somewhere for drinks and pizza before heading home. Pizza and alcohol had not been part of the menu served at Sophie's flat that evening, thus deepening an already puzzling mystery. Could it be that she had actually gone out with Rudy Guede that evening, at least long enough to have a few drinks and perhaps a slice of pizza? It was supposed to have been an open-and-shut case, *Caso chiuso*, but was now looking like anything but, and only served to further increase the frustration of the police and Meredith's family. Nonetheless Mignini, who had been claiming that 'the Americans' and others were attempting to 'destabilize' the investigation, stood by the case that had so far been built against the three suspects.

'We are more than happy with how things are proceeding,' Mignini said. 'The DNA of all three suspects is at the house, we have them at the scene, and one admits to being there, while Knox and Sollecito do not... Knox has made declarations which she has changed several times. This behaviour in itself is unusual and warrants holding her.

'First, she says she wasn't there, then she was and now she wasn't,' Mignini continued. 'Lies, all lies. Initially, we felt that all three were protecting each other and now [that] Sollecito and Knox are trying to push the blame on Guede, he has come out fighting and put the others at the scene. All three were involved in this murder. The question is how to attribute individual roles.'

On Friday, April 18, a hearing was called so that the new forensic report ordered by Judge Matteini could be discussed. Although it was designated a closed hearing, members of Meredith's family – mother Arline, sister Stephanie, and brother Lyle, who had travelled to

Perugia to attend – were allowed inside. Raffaele Sollecito was the only suspect to attend. It was the first time that Meredith's family, sitting only a few feet away, had come face-to-face with one of the suspects, and an icy chill seemed to pervade the courtroom.

Although several aspects of the hearing were difficult for Meredith's family to bear, they remained in court until graphic photographs of Meredith's body were shown. Too much for them to take, and clearly upset by what they had seen, they left for a brief time to recover their composure.

A day earlier, when they had first arrived in Perugia, the family paid a surprise visit to lead prosecutor Mignini to talk to him about the case. While it was not known what was said during the meeting, they did say later that they had full faith in the police investigation. After the meeting with Mignini, the family held a press conference.

'Generally we are pleased with the way the investigation has been going,' Lyle Kercher said. 'We have been a bit disappointed with some of the information that has been leaked, both in terms of the frequency and the content of it, none more so than of course the images and the video footage that was released a couple of weeks ago from the crime scene... this was in our opinion poor taste and unnecessary.'

He said that his family was confident that Meredith's killer or killers would be brought to justice when all was said and done.

'Ultimately, nothing can be done to undo what has happened and bring Meredith back,' he continued. 'All we can do is to hope we can work together to ensure that those responsible are brought to justice. Despite attempts to perhaps discredit evidence and undermine the process, we do have every faith in the police, forensic experts, the legal team that we have and the Italian justice system, and believe their efforts will ultimately see the right person or persons responsible suitably punished.'

Towards the end of the press conference, the Kercher family lawyer, Francesco Maresca, read a statement from the family to reporters: 'Almost six months since she died, we are still coming to terms with the idea of never seeing our Meredith smiling and happy again. We are here today and it is easier to see the motive as to why Meredith fell in love with Perugia and why she chose to study Italian here, with the prospect of maybe teaching or working in politics. Undoubtedly she would have chosen a career in which she would have made a difference.

'As you can see,' the statement continued, 'Meredith was particularly loved by all her family and friends, who have expressed their condolences and closeness in these months. The bright future that Mez had in front of her has been snatched away, but we want that her happy personality is remembered instead of a tragic event of which she was victim.'

As the three murder suspects languished in jail and Amanda continued to write in her prison diary, singing Beatles songs to herself to keep her spirits up, investigators continued studying the evidence, witness statements, and interviews with the suspects as they built their case. Finally, three months later, on Friday, July 11, Mignini was satisfied that he had what he needed to successfully prosecute the case in court and issued a formal request that Amanda Knox, Raffaele Sollecito, and Rudy Guede be charged with Meredith Kercher's murder and that the case be sent to trial. It was at that time that Mignini sent the file to Paolo Micheli, a preliminary hearing trial judge, who would decide whether there was sufficient evidence to bring the three suspects to trial or to release them without charge. Because the wheels of justice turn slowly in Italy, as does practically everything – which some may perceive as not necessarily a bad thing – it would probably take Micheli until mid-September to make such a determination.

'We knew this would happen, although we had hoped that the prosecutor would make further investigations,' said Raffaele's lawyer, Brusco. 'We especially wanted him to focus on CCTV footage from the car park opposite the house where poor Meredith was murdered, as this is vital. However, this was not the case, so we shall make a formal request at the preliminary hearing in September.'

Meanwhile, earlier in the week, Amanda celebrated

her 21st birthday within the confines of Capanne prison with her mother, Edda. Raffaele sent her a bouquet of flowers, but there was no birthday cake because it was not allowed by prison authorities.

CHAPTER 18

On Tuesday, September 9, 2008, a week before the scheduled preliminary hearing to decide if there was sufficient evidence to bring the three murder suspects to trial, Rudy Guede, in a surprise move through his lawyer, asked for a 'fast track' trial instead. According to attorneys Valter Biscotti and Nicodemo Gentile, the request was made because they, along with Guede, feared that a pact had been made between Amanda and Raffaele against their client.

'We feel the urgent need to have our trial heard independently of the other two suspects,' Biscotti said. 'In recent weeks a lot of poison has been spread by the defence teams and we feel the necessity to find some form of serenity in a separate hearing. That's why we have asked for a fast-track hearing just for our client, and we want that hearing as quickly as possible. At this hearing we will prove that our client has absolutely nothing to do with the tragic death of Meredith Kercher.'

According to Italian law, in a fast-track trial or hearing, no witnesses are called to testify and the evidence is presented by admitting documentation. The entire proceeding is conducted behind closed doors before a single judge who determines whether a defendant is innocent or guilty. A defendant who chooses this option is typically given one-third off of any sentence if found guilty.

'We have studied the evidence and there is no link between our client and the weapon found and which is said to be compatible with the wounds on Meredith Kercher,' Gentile said. 'It is up to the prosecution to prove that our client is guilty of murder, and in this case there is no evidence to back that up and there is the real risk of an innocent man being convicted.'

Biscotti released a letter that Guede had written from prison in which he again professed his innocence and said the only thing he was guilty of was not saving Meredith's life. He claimed the man he later identified as Raffaele, who had been rushing to leave the scene, had shouted at him in Italian, 'Black man found, black man guilty' – another reason he was opting for a fast-track trial.

'I can't find peace with myself because I am guilty of not doing what should have been done to save her, and I pray to God that justice will be had for her,' an excerpt from Guede's letter stated. 'It's easier for them to point the finger at me than at themselves because in their world that is what comes naturally rather than admitting your responsibilities... too many lies have been said about me, lies from certain individuals that make it clear to me that they want things hidden, they don't want things to come out... I have been described as a drug dealer and a drug addict and ask myself what the next thing I will be accused of is. Terrorism?'

The main pre-trial hearing began the following Tuesday, September 16, and would run more than a month before a decision would be made on whether or not to bring the suspects to trial or not. Meredith's parents, along with her sister, Stephanie, returned to Perugia to attend portions of the hearing. It would be the first time that they would encounter all three suspects together at one time. Before the hearing got underway, Stephanie gave reporters another statement about her sister.

'Each time that we arrive in Perugia,' she said, 'we wish it was for a different reason. It is so easy to understand why Meredith chose this beautiful city. She loved everything about Italy, but the fact that she chose Perugia over other cities shows how important the year abroad was for her. We only wish she'd had more time before she was brutally taken from us. We are pleased that we have reached a new phase in the process, hoping that justice will soon be done for Meredith.'

Defence lawyers and those critical of the handling

of the investigation had charged that to date the murder weapon had not been found, no real motive for the crime had been established, and none of the three suspects confessed to killing Meredith. Instead, the critics said, the police and the prosecution based their case on DNA evidence found at the crime scene, and the fact that Amanda and Raffaele had repeatedly changed their accounts of what happened that night.

At the hearing, which was the first time she had been seen in public for nearly a year, Amanda entered the courtroom dressed in a white blouse and jeans, flanked by two female prison guards, and reflected no emotion. Raffaele was noticeably absent, and it was said that he was feeling poorly and could not attend. Early in the proceedings, Amanda, in what seemed like a spontaneous decision, stood up and addressed the court.

'Good morning,' she said. 'I just want to say I am innocent. I didn't murder my friend, Meredith.'

Outside the courtroom Meredith's mother Arline was noticeably upset, and Detective Monica Napoleone, in charge of the murder squad, assisted her inside, where she was joined by her husband, John, and daughter, Stephanie. It seemed obvious throughout the day that Amanda was deliberately avoiding making eye contact with Meredith's family, as pointed out by Napoleone in remarks later.

'All the family was very brave and composed,' Napoleone said. 'They spent a long time looking straight at Knox, but she never once met their gaze.'

Much of the first day of the hearing was taken up with formalities, mainly legal, and by the end it did not seem that a lot had been accomplished. Shortly after that first day, hearing dates were scheduled to be held on Fridays and Saturdays, a common practice in Italy to help even out the caseloads of everyone involved, even though it took considerably longer to move the case along. Meanwhile, Guede's fast-track trial was approved, and it would be held in conjunction with the main hearing before Judge Micheli.

As one day followed another and September turned into October, the Kercher family's lawyer, Francesco Maresca, at one point requested that they be considered for damages if any of the three defendants were found guilty, a common practice under Italian law that would result in as much as £700,000 being awarded.

'We will argue that this was a particularly violent crime and that all three were present and responsible for her death,' Maresca said. 'As part of the argument we will also be making a claim for financial compensation to be paid by the defendants to Meredith's family for the suffering they have gone through. At this stage I am not prepared to say what that figure is. It can be anything from one euro to a hundred million euro, but I am not going to say anything before the case.'

At another point during the lengthy hearing, the prosecutor, Mignini, told Judge Paolo Micheli that

Meredith was murdered and that the suspects had made her death look like a burglary. He also accused Amanda of wielding the knife, and said that both Raffaele and Guede had played major parts in the murder.

'Knox held the knife and stabbed poor Meredith while the others held her down,' Mignini said. 'Sollecito had a knife on him, but he didn't use it. At the same time, Guede strangled her and also tried to sexually assault her.'

Amanda's lawyer, Luciano Ghirga, however, disagreed. 'This reconstruction is a huge fantasy,' Ghirga said. 'There is no proof.' Brusco, Raffaele's lawyer, added that Mignini's version of events was a 'fine fairytale'.

It was also shown during the hearing that Meredith had 47 separate wounds to her body. In addition to three wounds to her throat, she had cuts and bruises on her hands and face. The prosecution argued that some of the wounds had occurred as she attempted to defend herself. Mignini pointed out that he believed Amanda was the prime suspect because Meredith's body had been 'covered by a duvet, and only a woman would want to cover another naked woman's body.'

On the other hand, Amanda's lawyers said that there was 'not one shred of evidence' that linked her to Meredith's murder, and argued that the evidence against her was 'insufficient and contradictory'. They also said that the knife police believed to be the murder weapon was the wrong size and did not match the evidence, such as the stain of a knife's image left in blood on one of the bed sheets.

Later, outside the courtroom during one of the breaks, the Kercher family lawyer said that he had ultimately asked for £20 million in damages from the three suspects if they are convicted, and outlined his reasons for asking for that amount.

'Poor Meredith suffered a painful, slow death,' Maresca said. 'She was dying... and went through a horrific ordeal. The three had no option but to kill her. Once they had started they could not turn back. They had to kill her because otherwise she would have gone to the police and told them about what had happened in the house... those bruises and wounds on Meredith's body are a sign of what she went through. She was virtually tortured before being killed in the end because of what had started as an erotic game... I have spoken with the Kercher family and they are being kept constantly informed about what is happening. They just want justice to be done, for Meredith and the truth.'

Back inside the courtroom, Amanda's lawyers stated that the knife blade that had caused the fatal wound was not as large as prosecutors had contended, and argued that the DNA found on the blade implicating Amanda was so small that it was insignificant.

'As far as we're concerned,' Ghirga said, 'Amanda Knox was not at the scene and was not responsible for

Meredith's murder. For us there was one aggressor, but I am not going to say who that was.'

Another lawyer on Amanda's legal team, Carlo Dalla Vedova, told the judge, as well as reporters later, that the evidence against Amanda was contradictory and insignificant.

'That is why we have asked… not to continue with this case against our client,' Dalla Vedova said to reporters. 'There is not enough proof for Amanda Knox to be sent for a full trial. She has made no confession. We are hopeful that the judge will accept this decision. Amanda did not speak at this hearing, but she is very stressed out by all these events. She did not kill Meredith – she was her friend. She is hopeful that the legal system will see this and she will be released.'

In Guede's fast-track trial, lawyers told the judge that their client did not know Amanda and Raffaele at the time of the murder, and that he was not at Meredith's cottage that night to 'rob, rape and kill her', as he had been accused. Instead, he was there 'to court her'. That, of course, was contradictory to what the Albanian witness had told police much earlier, namely that he had seen Amanda, Raffaele and Guede together outside the cottage on the night before Meredith was killed.

Guede's lawyers also again pointed out that 'the accusations are to be expected because he is an easy target. But he has never changed his story while the other two have.'

Of course, most of the facts – if not all – as they had been so far explored were examined at length during the hearing. When Mignini summed up his case, however, he emphasized the discovery of the violent Japanese *manga* comic books found in Raffaele's flat and pointed out that they depicted the murder 'of female vampires on Halloween night,' showing naked women lying dead on the floor with blood on the walls. He added that the depictions were chillingly similar to what police officers saw when they found Meredith's body. Mignini also said that he believed that the trio of suspects had intended to murder Meredith on Halloween night – 24 hours before she was murdered – but for reasons not known had put it off until the following night. The prosecutor said that Meredith and her friends had gone to a party on Halloween night dressed as vampires.

By the end of Mignini's summation he had asked that Guede be sentenced to life in prison at his fast-track trial, if granted, and that Amanda and Raffaele be sent for full trial.

Judge Micheli granted Mignini's request to send Amanda and Raffaele to full trial on charges of murder and sexual assault. He also convicted Guede that same day of murder and sexual assault, and sentenced him to 30 years in prison. Guede appealed asgainst his conviction and, on 22nd December 2009, his sentence was cut to 16 years.

Amanda and her parents became emotional when

Judge Micheli had announced his decisions. They had been convinced that Amanda would be freed from custody at the conclusion of the pre-trial hearing and cried when they realized that had not happened.

'I spent a lot of time crying last night,' Edda Mellas said on a U.S. television news programme. 'I just worry about her and the toll this is all going to take on her, on her life... Amanda's lawyers told her that this is what happens with most Italian pre-trials – there are very few that are totally dismissed, and they continued to tell her, "You're innocent. We will have to go to court but you will be found innocent." I don't fear that they are going to find her guilty. There's no evidence, no motive, nothing.'

'We had high hopes that the evidence brought forth would be enough to allow this case to be dismissed,' Amanda's father said. 'We are very disappointed... Amanda is anything but the type of personality that they are portraying for this whole scenario. She is 180 degrees different than the type of person that would get into a position that they are describing.'

Mignini, of course, was pleased with Judge Micheli's decisions, particularly Guede's conviction. Mignini remained convinced, however, that Guede could not have acted alone.

At the time of writing, Guede is appealing his conviction.

CHAPTER 19

During Rudy Guede's fast-track trial and afterwards, as Amanda and Raffaele along with their lawyers prepared for the start of their trial, which was expected to run for about a year, there was renewed public interest in the sex life of 'Foxy Knoxy', as Amanda was nicknamed – in part because the reading public seemingly had not yet had enough of it. *Daily Mail* reporter Nick Pisa, who had followed the case closely from its outset, revealed that a number of conversations between Amanda and her parents had been leaked to the press. During those conversations Amanda, who shared a cell with a woman named Rosa, a convicted murderer, told her parents that her cellmate begged her for sex. The conversations between Amanda and her parents were taped by prison officials who had placed a recording bug in the visiting room. Amanda said that Rosa 'whispered to me one night if I would like to have sex with her.'

'It's because I'm pretty and they all like me,' Amanda added.

Amanda also told her parents that Rosa was serving a 25-year sentence on the murder conviction, but that Amanda thinks 'she is innocent'. She also said that there were a number of Nigerian prostitutes in her area of the prison who 'are actually quite nice'. She said that she helped Rosa clean their cell, and complained that it had resulted in rough chapped hands and broken fingernails.

'Rosa makes me clean the cell the whole time,' she said. 'She is a fanatic. She spends the whole day cleaning and scrubbing and she makes me do it as well.'

Around the middle of November 2008 a new twist in the case occurred – witnesses, previously unknown to prosecutors and police, began to come forward. The first claimed he saw Amanda shopping in the cleaning section of a convenience store, located near Raffaele's flat, a few hours before Meredith's body was discovered. The purported sighting had occurred during the time-frame that Amanda had claimed to have been at Raffaele's flat. The witness provided his statement to prosecutors Giuliano Mignini and Manuela Comodi, after which details appeared in the local newspaper *Giornale dell'Umbria*.

The statement seemed to support evidence recovered by detectives from Raffaele's apartment during a search after the murder, including a receipt from the store where the witness said that he had seen

Amanda. The detectives had also found a bleach bottle and cloths under a sink at the flat, which they believe were used to clean a knife or knives, as well as the murder scene itself.

'That morning I saw Amanda at 7.45,' the witness said. 'She was wearing a grey hooded jacket, zipped up to the top, jeans and a grey-blue scarf which was wrapped around her face. She also wore a light-coloured hat. I know it was her. I had seen her in the Corso Garibaldi. I know Sollecito by sight and in the days before the murder I saw the American girl with him.' Corso Garibaldi is the name of the street where Raffaele's flat was located.

'I had looked at them closely because I always used to see Sollecito on his own,' the witness added. 'That's why it struck me... I recognized Amanda Knox from the photographs in the newspapers and on the TV. I told some friends that the day the body was found she was out shopping early in the morning.'

Although it was not clear why the witness, whose name was not immediately released, had waited so long to come forward with the information, he told the prosecutors that he thought it had been 'very strange' for a student to be out so early in the day.

'She was also acting very strange,' the witness said. 'That morning was virtually a holiday, as there were no lectures. If there had been, I could understand her being up so early. She was acting suspiciously. She had covered her face – that's why I couldn't get a good look at it. It was as if she didn't want to be recognized. She didn't say hello and she didn't look me in the eye.'

The witness described Amanda as being about 1.65 metres tall, with light-coloured eyes. Although he did not know whether she had actually purchased anything from the store, he said that he saw her go 'to the section of the shop that sells cleaning products.'

Although Amanda's lawyers were unavailable for comment after news of the witness surfaced, Kercher family lawyer Francesco Maresca said that he had heard about it. 'What he has to say appears to be very significant,' Maresca said. 'It puts Knox out much earlier than she claimed to the police and is very important to the case.'

A few days later another witness, a 40-year-old man, came forward and reported having seen Amanda, Raffaele, and Rudy Guede together on October 30, 2007, two days before Meredith was killed. The new evidence again challenged Amanda and Raffaele's statements in which they had claimed they did not know Rudy Guede.

Before the month had ended, yet another witness told authorities of having seen a cut or scratch on Amanda's neck shortly after Meredith's body had been discovered. This latest witness was Laura Mezzetti, one of Amanda and Meredith's flatmates, who said she noticed the cut when she and Amanda were discussing the tragedy. Mezzetti had not mentioned the cut during initial interviews with police, but the information came out when she was called in and questioned again.

The police and prosecutors had also evidently missed seeing the purported cut. After Mezzetti's latest statement, Mignini asked to see the medical records of Amanda's examination at the time of her arrest. He wanted to see if the cut had been noted.

'The flatmate's recollection of the scratch on Amanda Knox's throat is very significant,' said a source from the prosecutor's office. 'Was it there as a result of attempts by Meredith to defend herself? The flatmate did not mention it at the time because she did not think it was important and she remembered it recently and, as a result, mentioned it to the prosecution. Medical evidence from the time is being examined to see if there was any mention of this scratch on Knox's neck.'

Another witness interviewed during the latest round of questioning as the prosecution prepared its witness list for the court was Amy Frost, a British student also studying in Perugia and Meredith's best friend. She provided an interesting, if not suspicious, account of her encounter with Raffaele at the police station while they and a number of other people waited to be questioned by detectives. She said that he had simply approached and began talking about his and Amanda's activities during the time-frame when Meredith was believed killed.

'He came up to me and said, "I am Raffaele,

Amanda's boyfriend",' Frost related. ' "Amanda was at my house last night with me. She didn't leave until 10.30 this morning. When she got back she found the apartment with the door open." He just carried on without me asking him anything.'

Just about everyone associated with the case knew that there would be a multitude of books about it rushing to press. Most assumed the books would be published after the trial. However, to many people's surprise, the first book hit bookstore shelves before the end of November 2008. It was called *Amanda and the Others*, and was written by Fiorenza Sarzanini, described as one of Italy's leading crime journalists. Sarzanini portrayed Amanda as a young woman for whom sex was a main ingredient of her life. Some of the information about Amanda's sex life was taken from her diary.

'Knox isn't obsessed with sex, but she sees it as one of the predominant aspects of her life,' Sarzanini said during an interview with the British newspaper the *The Sunday Times*. 'This has influenced her life in the sense that it influences her relationships with both men and women.'

Sarzanini's book named four men in Seattle and New York, and three in Florence and Perugia, with whom Amanda had had sex.

'It's as if [Knox] was always hunting men,' Sarzanini said. 'You list your conquests as if you were displaying them like trophies.'

In one section of the book Sarzanini wrote about the day Amanda arrived at the cottage in Perugia, and quoted testimony that Amy Frost, Meredith's friend, had given to police.

'Meredith told us that Amanda put down in the bathroom a beauty case in which there were condoms and a vibrator,' Frost had said. 'They were visible and it seemed a bit strange to Meredith.' Meredith later told Frost, 'Isn't it odd that a girl arrives and the first thing she shows is a vibrator?'

Sarzanini also wrote about how Frost had noticed tension between Meredith and Amanda when Meredith told her how one of the guys living in the lower half of the cottage, Giacomo Silenzi, fancied her. Amanda purportedly replied that she liked Giacomo, too, but that Meredith could have him. Frost said that Amanda's remark had upset her, but she had gone on to start a relationship with the young man anyway.

Another segment of the book claimed that Amanda wanted to write a song about Meredith's murder, right after Meredith's body had been found.

'So I am at the police station after a long day in which I describe how I was the first person to arrive home and find my flatmate dead,' read an excerpt from Amanda's diary. 'The strange thing is after all that has happened, I want to write a song about all this. It would be the first song I have written and would speak about how someone died in a horrible way and for no reason.'

Amanda also wrote that she was 'feeling so hungry I could murder a pizza... How morbid is all that? I'm dying of hunger. I really want to say that I could murder a pizza but that doesn't seem right. Laura and Filomena are really upset. I'm angry. At the beginning I was shocked, then sad, then confused, now I'm really angry. I don't know. I never saw her body and I never saw her blood so it's as if it hasn't happened. But it did happen, right in the room next to mine. There was blood in the bathroom where this morning I took a shower.'

These and other excerpts from the book were published in the magazine supplement of *Corriere Della Sera*, a leading daily Italian newspaper where Sarzanini also worked. Its cover consisted of a digitally enhanced photo of Amanda that had been designed to depict her as cold and calculating, with a caption below it which read: 'Amanda's Nights. Alcohol, Drugs and Sex.'

Amanda's parents were of course outraged over the revelations contained in the book, as well as the article about it, as were many of the murder suspect's other supporters, and said that it was unfortunate that Amanda's private and personal property had been made public in a book.

'We have not seen the source of the information and have no way to judge its authenticity, whether information has been quoted accurately, whether it exists at all, and whether or not it is being reported in proper context,' Curt Knox and Edda Mellas said in a statement released to the news media. 'This seems to be yet another example of the continued leaks of information designed to harm Amanda's character, as there is no evidence to tie her to the brutal and senseless murder of Meredith Kercher. She is innocent.'

Although the trial had been scheduled to begin in early December 2008, it was delayed until mid-January 2009 to allow officials additional time to prepare their documentation. In the meantime, Amanda moved to have her case thrown out after learning about Sarzanini's book, claiming that it had damaged her chance of getting a fair trial. The book had been a bestseller in Italy and had been serialized in the *Corriere Della Sera* and had, therefore, been read by a large number of people, and it reportedly had been a very popular Christmas 2008 gift. In addition to wanting the case against her dismissed, Amanda wanted £500,000 in damages. Amanda had also filed a request through her lawyer, Carlo Dalla Vedova, with the Milan Civil Court that the book be seized.

'There is no doubt that this book will have an impact on my client's trial,' Dalla Vedova said. 'That is why we have made this request and also claimed damages.'

As she defended her book, Sarzanini said that she had relied on excerpts from Amanda's diary which had been seized by the police after her arrest a year earlier. Sarzanini said that the diary was part of the evidence against Amanda, and that the sexual elements her book contained had been established already in earlier judicial proceedings.

'In my book I used the diary written by Amanda Knox herself and which is now part of the evidence in the trial against her,' Sarzanini said. 'I don't understand how the fact that I have retold her own words in a book can have a negative influence on her trial.'

Meanwhile, Kercher family lawyer Francesco Maresca announced that he was requesting that the trial be held behind closed doors. 'This is something I have discussed with the family of poor Meredith,' Maresca said. 'We are talking about a sex crime and we don't want to turn it into some morbid spectacle. During the hearings last month we had more than 200 journalists and if we have that many again at the trial it will be chaos. I will be requesting that just three or four at the most are present on a rotation basis. The final decision will be up to the judge, but I want to try and avoid cameras and photographers pointing at Meredith's family who will be in court for the trial.'

CHAPTER 20

The trial of Amanda Knox and Raffaele Sollecito finally began on Friday, January 16, 2009 before presiding Judge Giancarlo Massei. As had been the case during earlier proceedings, most, if not all, trial days would occur on Fridays and Saturdays. When Amanda Knox entered the packed courtroom she was all smiles as she made her way through a gauntlet of people towards the defence table. Her attorney, Luciano Ghirga, gave her a pat on the back as she walked past him.

Before the proceedings officially commenced, a number of journalists, upset over the cramped conditions in the courtroom and the fact that their view was obscured by TV cameras, staged a protest by entering barred cages normally reserved for Mafia suspects or terrorists. They were eventually instructed to take their places.

The eight-member jury consisted of two judges plus three women and three men, and was sworn in by Judge Massei, as Amanda smiled, and sometimes smirked, from her place at the defence table. Raffaele pointedly never exchanged glances with Amanda from his place in the courtroom, but Amanda frequently looked at him and smiled.

Judge Massei ruled against Maresca's motion to keep the proceedings closed for the sake of the Kercher family, but reserved the right to exclude reporters and photographers when necessary. Major trials are typically televised in Italy, but Massei sided with the prosecution argument that cameras in court could potentially capture shots of photos of Meredith's body from evidence being presented and ruled that television and press cameras would not be allowed after the start of the proceedings – they could be there to capture the preliminary 'housework', but not after the trial got under way. Massei indicated such measures were necessary to protect Meredith's dignity and memory.

Amanda and Raffaele were each charged with sexual assault, which carries a sentence of 6-12 years; theft, 1-6 years; simulation of a crime, 1-3 years; possession of a weapon, up to 1 year; and murder with cruelty, a life sentence. Amanda was also charged with slander for accusing the police of striking her, as well as saying they physically and psychologically intimidated her during the interrogation. Police had testified that no one had harmed her while in police custody. Her so-called confession about her presence at the crime scene at the time of the murder had been declared inadmissible because, the court ruled, she did not have a lawyer present during questioning.

In early February 2009, during the first day that evidence was presented, Raffaele looked nervous at times and Amanda seemed intent on chewing her fingernails as the court was told that the couple looked 'embarrassed and surprised' when the first officers arrived at the murder scene, after Meredith's mobile phone had been found in a neighbour's garden. Inspector Michele Battistelli said: 'They were whispering to each other and told me they were waiting for the Carabinieri. They didn't say when they had called them, just that they were waiting for them. They told me that they had come back to the house and found the front door open and the window of one of the flatmates, Filomena Romanelli, smashed.'

Battistelli added that he went inside with Amanda and Raffaele, and they showed him the broken window and the ransacked room with clothes strewn about on the floor. He said that he noted that the glass was lying on top of the clothing articles, which suggested to him that the window had been broken after the clothes had been tossed about on the floor.

'I immediately thought that this had been an attempt to make it look like a break-in,' he said. 'I told the two accused this but they didn't answer me. I also noticed that there was a laptop on the bedroom table and a camera in the kitchen, items that would have been taken during a break-in.'

He then decided to break down the door to Meredith's room.

'At this time Knox and Sollecito were not here,' he said. 'They were away from the scene. Romanelli's boyfriend gave the door three kicks and it opened. I was behind him and heard a scream. I looked and when I saw the scene I told everyone to get out. There was blood everywhere, a lot, but I did not go in. I then called the operations room.'

Battistelli said that he had 'some idea' of how Meredith had died from what he had quickly observed – he said that he had seen marks on her neck as well as the blood. He said that he did not speak to anyone about it, prompting prosecutors to point out that when Amanda was at the police station waiting to be questioned she had spoken about the injuries to Meredith's body which, Mignini said, 'only the killers would know about.'

The court also heard testimony from Filomena Romanelli that neither Raffaele nor Amanda had shed a tear when Meredith's body was discovered, while most of the others present at the scene did. She also recalled for the court how Amanda had telephoned her earlier that morning to say, 'There's something strange in the house. The door is open and there's some blood.'

Robyn Butterworth also testified, and said that Amanda's behaviour that day at the cottage had been 'very strange'.

'Everybody was really upset but she didn't seem to show any emotion about what had happened or any thought for anyone else who was there,' Butterworth said. She went on to describe how Amanda had sat with her feet on Raffaele's lap, and had considered their behaviour 'upsetting' considering the circumstances.

'They were kissing and joking together,' Butterworth said. 'I remember Amanda sticking her tongue out at Raffaele.' Butterworth also testified that when one of their other friends had said she hoped that Meredith had not suffered, Amanda responded with, 'What do you think? She fucking bled to death.'

On Wednesday, February 18, while the trial was in recess during one of its many 'off' days, police in Perugia made a startling discovery that quickly made news, first throughout Italy and then across the world. They had discovered that the house in which Meredith Kercher had been sexually assaulted and murdered more than a year earlier had been broken into and ransacked, presumably by devil worshippers, despite the best efforts to keep the house sealed off as a crime scene. The house and its perimeter had been marked with police tape ever since the murder, but sentries were no longer guarding it as of January 2009. Since the house had been left unguarded, police were uncertain as to when the break-in actually occurred. The intrusion, police said, had been discovered when officers returned some items to the house that had been seized earlier as part of the investigation into Meredith's murder.

With satanic worship apparently somewhat widespread in Italy over the past several years, murder scenes are often used to carry out unholy ceremonies. Some people believed that because there had been a great deal of blood at the crime scene, coupled with the fact that Meredith's body had been partially nude, these factors may have contributed to the house having possibly been selected by Satanists for their rituals.

Among the oddities discovered by investigators following up on the break-in were four knives on the kitchen floor, as well as a burned out candle in another room and candle wax drippings in the room where Meredith was slain. Nothing appeared to be missing from the house. According to police, the intruders' point of entry was through a kitchen window at the rear of the house.

'Four knives were found at the scene, and they were all determined to be from inside the house,' said a spokesperson for the police. 'They were not brought here. A candle was also found, but this also appears to have already been in the house. Traces of wax were found in Meredith's bedroom and at this stage we are keeping an open mind on the motive. We cannot exclude anything, and it is possible that it was for some unnatural reason, such as Satanism.'

'I have no words to describe how much distress this will cause the family,' Maresco said. 'I hope that the full details about what happened will come out quickly.'

Marco Brusco, Raffaele's attorney, viewed the break-in as possibly being beneficial to his client's case. 'This break-in just shows what we have always said – anyone could get into the house,' Brusco said. 'It proves how easy it is to get into the house and tamper with the crime scene... we are very concerned about what happened, but at the same time it proves what we have always said – that a thief broke into the house and murdered poor Meredith Kercher.'

To date, the mysterious break-in, amid suspicions of satanic activity, remains a mystery.

As the trial continued and February drew to a close, testimony was given by Monica Napoleone, head of Perugia's homicide squad, who described a woman's shoe print found on a pillow beneath Meredith's body. Because the size of the shoe print, between size 36 to 38, was compatible with Amanda's shoe size, 37, it had been viewed as suspicious but had not yet been matched to any specific shoe belonging to Amanda.

Napoleone also described Amanda's behaviour that day at the police station, and characterized it as unusual. She said at one point Amanda had complained about being tired, and Napoleone told her that she could leave.

'She said she wanted to stay,' Napoleone said. 'Sollecito was also at the police station at the time and she said she wanted to wait for him. A few minutes later I walked past a room at the police station where she was waiting and I saw Amanda doing the splits and a cartwheel... she and Sollecito had a bizarre attitude throughout the whole time. They were laughing, kissing and pulling faces at each other... the flatmates and the British friends were very upset but Knox and Sollecito seemed to be more interested in each other. They were very indifferent to the situation and I found it quite disturbing, considering that the body of a young girl had been found in such terrible circumstances.'

In response to questions about Amanda's accusations of police brutality and statements that she had not been treated well by the police, Napoleone responded that she had been treated 'very well'.

'She was given water, chamomile tea and breakfast as well, and she was given cakes from a vending machine and then taken to the canteen at the police station for something to eat,' Napoleone testified.

Police officer Giacinto Profazio told the court that he, too, had observed a 'strange attitude' with Amanda and Raffaele. He said that Amanda had sat on Raffaele's knee at the police station, and that he had told both of them what he thought of their behaviour.

'She was in a room at the police station sitting on his knee,' Profazio testified. 'I told them it was not appropriate. I was also told that she did the splits and cartwheels in one of the rooms at the station. Then after being questioned, she burst into tears.'

Profazio also testified about being told that the broken window at the house may have been used by an intruder to gain entry, and shared his thoughts about such a scenario with the jury.

'I thought it strange,' Profazio said, 'as it would have needed a superhuman effort to climb up to it. There was a much easier way in at the back, via a terrace and a boiler. There was a chair and table on the terrace and it would have been a lot easier to get in this way.'

Profazio also took the judge and jury through much of the other evidence, including DNA, the knife, the fact that Amanda and Raffaele's mobile phones had been turned off at practically the same time the night of the murder, and so forth.

In March, the jurors heard testimony about how Amanda and Meredith had been involved in a row over money, and they were shown CCTV footage from the nearby car park the night Meredith was killed in a series of black-and-white photographs depicting a female figure with long hair, believed to have been Meredith, walking down the slope towards the cottage. The time stamp on the footage indicated that it had been at 8.41 p.m., according to testimony by police inspector Mauro Barbadori.

'From the time on the film and the fact it is a female figure, the belief is that it is Meredith, but it is very poor quality and we cannot say for definite,' Barbadori said. 'Hypothetically speaking it is very possible that the figure seen is Meredith returning home after spending the evening at a friend's house.'

After hearing from the witness who reported seeing Amanda out shopping for cleaning products when she had claimed to be in bed, another witness, Nara Capezzali, 68, testified about hearing a terrifying scream that came from the house where Meredith was killed.

'I went to bed around 9-9.30 p.m. as there was nothing on the TV and I woke up around two hours later to go to the bathroom,' Capezzali said. 'On my way I passed by the window and heard a scream, not a normal scream but a prolonged scream. It made my skin crawl. I didn't know what was happening. I looked out the window but didn't see anything. Then a few minutes later I heard running on the metal staircase [near the street] and then running through the leaves going in the other direction. It was at least two people. The scream left me really disturbed, and even now it troubles me. It was a woman's scream – there was no call for help, it was a scream and then nothing.'

Capezzali then demonstrated the scream she heard for the court's benefit.

Other witnesses gave testimony to having seen both Amanda and Raffaele together that night, outside the crime scene. At another point, when photos of Meredith's injuries were shown, Amanda averted and shielded her eyes, unable to look at the images. The court was also told that an attempt had been made to strangle Meredith before she was fatally stabbed in the throat with two different knives.

On Friday, June 6, Meredith Kercher's family returned to Perugia to attend the trial. Her mother, Arline, fighting back tears, told the court that she would never get over the 'brutality' of her daughter's death and said that she desperately missed Meredith, who she described as 'conscientious'. When she spoke it was often between taking deep breaths, an attempt to keep from crying.

'Her death was unbelievable, unreal,' she said. 'In many ways, it still is. I still look for her. It's not just her death but it is the nature of it, the brutality of it, the violence of it and the great sorrow it's brought everyone. It is such a shock to send your child to school and for them to not come back. We will never, never get over it.'

Mrs Kercher became visibly moved when asked to recall her final telephone conversation with Meredith. She said that they spoke by phone every day, mainly to discuss Meredith's plans for her next return to England. The last time had been on the afternoon of November 1, only hours before she was murdered.

'She rang to let me know when she was coming back,' she testified. 'She said she was really tired because they had been out for Halloween the night before and they had come back very late and she was going to see some friends to see a film. But she was coming back early – she had an essay to finish.'

She explained that Meredith had lectures to attend at the university the following morning, and exams were fast approaching. Describing her daughter as a 'hard working' student, she said that Meredith had never expressed any fears or concerns about her life in Perugia, but had often talked of how much she loved it there. She said that Meredith had chosen Perugia because it was 'small', had 'good airport links', and because she loved its chocolate festival held in the autumn.

A week later, during the trial's next Friday-Saturday session, Amanda would take the witness stand to testify for the first time in her murder trial. On Friday, June 12, she told the court about her seven lovers and how she had been led to believe that she was HIV-positive, and how being told that she might have AIDS had scared her.

'They told me it was positive and they said I had AIDS,' she testified. 'I was left shocked. I didn't know how that could be possible. They told me to think about it hard and so I wrote in my diary about all the partners I'd had.'

'How many partners did you have?' asked Dalla Vedova, her attorney.

'Seven,' she replied. 'I was going through them and saying 'I made love to him, well he can't have it and he can't have it'... I was really worried. *Mamma mia*, I was crying. I thought I was going to die and not be able to have any children. They took the test three times over two weeks and I was under so much pressure because I thought I had AIDS.'

At one point she described how a doctor had found a mark on her neck during her in-processing medical examination after being arrested. As she spoke, a large cold sore was visible on the outside of her upper lip.

'It was a hickey,' she said. 'A love bite from Raffaele.'

When asked why she had blamed Patrick Lumumba for Meredith's murder, Amanda explained that she had felt pressured by the police and claimed that she had been beaten by officers prior to making false statements against her will. Lumumba was in the packed courtroom watching the proceedings.

'I was confused,' she added. 'The declarations were taken against my will, so everything I said was said in a state of confusion and under pressure.'

She said that the police had struck her twice on the back of her head during the interrogation.

'All the police were in the room,' she said. 'There were some behind me, some in front, and one of them shouted, "You don't remember?" then a policewoman behind me hit me across the back of the head. They called me a stupid liar and they said that I was trying to protect someone. But I was not trying to protect anyone. I didn't know how to respond to them. I was very, very scared because they were treating me so badly and I didn't understand why.'

She said that at one point during the interrogation a police officer confronted her with a text message that she had sent to Lumumba that said, 'See you later,' and held it in front of her face while demanding: 'Look, look at this message. You were going to meet someone.'

'I could not understand why they were so sure that I knew everything,' she continued. 'So in my confusion I started to imagine that maybe I was traumatized. They were suggesting a path to me – under pressure I imagined a lot of different things.'

When asked why she had performed splits and cartwheels at the police station, she responded that it had been her way of relaxing and 'lightening' the situation. When asked to describe the night of the murder, she said that she had seen Meredith that afternoon at the cottage.

'She left her room, said 'bye,' and walked out the door,' Amanda said. 'That was the last time I saw her.' That night, she said, she smoked a marijuana joint, had sex with Raffaele at his flat, and fell asleep afterwards.

Wearing jeans and a white blouse, Amanda Knox took the witness stand again the next day, and again spoke of the verbal and physical bullying she claimed police officers had subjected her to during long hours of interrogation.

'The police officers interrogating me said they would put me in prison for 30 years for being a liar,' she said. Cross-examined by prosecutors, she said that a 'crescendo' of police badgering and pressure had caused her to wrongly name an innocent man, and again talked of how a policewoman had struck her on the back of the head during questioning.

'It was always a crescendo,' she told Mignini about her early interrogation sessions. 'When I said I was with Raffaele all the time, they told me I was a liar. I was scared. I thought, maybe they are right.'

She said that her interrogators kept telling her that they 'wanted a name,' and that was when the policewoman would hit her twice on the head. She said that it was the pressure from the police that caused her to give them Lumumba's name.

'It didn't hurt,' she said of the policewoman striking her head. 'But it frightened me.'

CHAPTER 21

Later in the month of June 2009, Amanda's mother, Edda Mellas, testified that her daughter and Meredith Kercher 'got on great' and said that there had been no problems between the two, a contradiction of sorts to what other witnesses had said throughout the investigation and in court. During two hours of sometimes emotional testimony, with the help of an interpreter, Mellas said that Amanda had never even considered leaving Italy to return to the U.S. after the murder because she wanted to remain there to 'help the authorities and continue her studies'.

'They got along great,' Mellas said. 'Amanda told me about the fun things she and Meredith did.'

Although Mellas did not elaborate about the 'fun things', she went on to testify about three phone calls she received from Amanda on November 2, 2007, the morning Meredith's body was found.

'In her first call, she said she thought somebody was in the house,' Mellas said, adding that the second and third calls were made after Meredith's body had been found. 'She was very upset. It was very disturbing.'

Two weeks later, at trial sessions in early July, Professor Carlo Torre, a leading forensic expert, testified on behalf of the defence about two knives the police said were used in the murder. Using a mannequin head, Torre showed the court how the wounds found on Meredith's neck were incompatible with a 30 cm knife which the police said had been found in Raffaele's flat. The media and the public were asked to leave during part of Torre's testimony because graphic photos of Meredith's body were used and shown to the court.

'Examining the blade found, and the wounds, it is clear that it [the knife blade] is incompatible,' Torre said. 'It is my opinion that the blade that caused the wounds to the victim's neck was much shorter, probably around 8 centimetres, and that it was no more than a centimetre wide. The knife went in and out of the wounds, once, twice, three times, in a sawing motion.'

Professor Torre also pointed out that Meredith's hyoid bone, a small bone in the neck, had been broken after considerable pressure had been applied to it – an indication of strangulation. Torre, who examined the video made of the crime scene, the video of the autopsy on Meredith's body, and the accompanying pathologist's notes, said that there was 'nothing to make me think that more than one person was involved... there are no elements or traces to suggest anyone else was involved.'

Torre talked about blood splatter on Meredith's chest, and said that she was not wearing a bra. He said the blood spots were compatible with having been 'breathed out' as she died. He said that the bruises found on her body did not necessarily indicate that she had been held down during the attack, but had been caused by her thrashing around, 'bashing and knocking' into the floor and the furniture.

Following a lengthy summer break of approximately two months, Amanda and Raffaele's trial resumed in mid-September 2009 amid a defence motion to dismiss the charges against the two defendants because of alleged faulty forensic work. The defence teams argued that DNA evidence was invalid and said that the case should be dismissed due to the alleged 'unreliability of the DNA results'.

Judge Massei, however, refused the request and said that the tests had been performed correctly and that the 'defendants' rights had not been harmed'.

Later, prosecutors brought in a knife wrapped in plastic and showed it to the jury and asserted that it could have been the knife used to kill Meredith. It was the knife found at Raffaele's flat. Three forensic experts were called by his defence team to discuss the alleged murder weapon. Raffaele's lawyers argued that the knife was too large to match the wounds on Meredith's neck. They also argued that the amount of Meredith's DNA found on the knife was too minute to be admitted into evidence. One of the three forensic experts for the defence, Mariano Cingolani, provided information intended to cast doubt on the knife's compatibility with one of the wounds on Meredith's neck, but not the wound that was considered to be the fatal one. 'Many other knives in general are more compatible with that kind of wound,' Cingolani said.

One of the three cuts on Meredith's neck would have been larger if the prosecution's knife had been used, he maintained. Cingolani also said that no firm conclusion could be reached without knowing the position that Meredith's neck had been in during the attack or the elasticity of the tissues in her neck.

The following month, November 2009, Rudy Guede was brought back into the courtroom to provide testimony at the start of his appeal hearing. He took the court through the details of how he had met Meredith at a Halloween party in Perugia in October 2007, and how he had gone to her cottage the next day. He said that he and Meredith had talked and kissed, but had decided not to have sex.

He repeated his account of how Meredith had complained about her missing money, and how she had blamed Amanda and accused her of taking it.

'"My money, my money,"' he quoted Meredith as saying. '"I can't stand her."'

He said that Meredith also complained about Amanda's personal habits and how she brought men back to the cottage. He then went into the details of how he had gone into the bathroom with his iPod, and a few minutes later he had heard shouting between Meredith and Amanda.

'They were discussing the missing money,' Guede testified. 'I heard Meredith say, "We need to talk." Then I heard a loud scream. It was above the volume of the [iPod] music. I came out and went into Meredith's bedroom and I saw a male silhouette. I saw Meredith on the floor and this person tried to hit me. I fell over and this person ran out and I heard them say, "Let's go, there's a Negro here". I went into the corridor and looking out of the window I saw going away the outline of Amanda Knox.'

Prosecutor Pietro Catalani said that Guede's account was 'worthy of a fairytale.'

'We are expected to believe he flirted with Meredith, then all this happens in the space of a few minutes while he is in the bathroom?' Catalani asked the court. Catalani added how traces of Guede's DNA had been found inside the cottage and on Meredith's body.

Guede's appeal concluded on 22nd December 2009, and his sentence was cut from 30 to 16 years for the murder. In a statement Valter Biscotti, his lawyer, said that Guede was not happy about the reduction because 'he is innocent'. A second appeal against his conviction is planned.

As the end of Amanda and Raffaele's trial drew near, they remained optimistic and confident that they would be found innocent, as did their families. Their lawyers, however, had asked for an independent review of all the evidence because of the uncertainties that many people, including experts, had expressed about it and the way it was handled. However, the court denied the request for the review.

On Saturday, November 21, Mignini told the court during closing arguments that Amanda Knox had a growing hatred for Meredith Kercher and had 'killed her to take revenge' during an evening fuelled by drugs. Mignini said that Amanda, Raffaele, and Guede had killed Meredith after becoming intoxicated by 'the fumes of drugs and possibly alcohol,' because Amanda had wanted revenge against Meredith for saying that she had poor hygiene and was promiscuous. He asserted that the trio had then attempted to cover their crime by staging a burglary.

'Amanda had the chance to retaliate against a girl who was serious and quiet,' Mignini said. 'She harboured hatred for Meredith. That was the time it could explode. The time had come to take revenge on that smirky girl.'

Mignini said that the trio met at the cottage where

Amanda and Meredith lived, and that the two girls began arguing before Amanda, Raffaele, and Guede brutally attacked Meredith.

'Meredith and Amanda began to argue over money,' Mignini said. 'Meredith was upset that Amanda had brought another man [Guede] back to the house. They argued about this ugly habit of hers and the three who had arrived were also under the influence of drugs and alcohol. Amanda harboured hatred for Meredith and the time had come for her to take revenge, and that's when Meredith's ordeal began... Amanda grabbed her by the hair and hit her head on the floor. Rudy finished what he did and Sollecito was threatening her with his knife. Amanda also had a knife and held it to Meredith's throat, and as the crescendo of violence grew, inflicted the deepest cut. Meredith did not want to submit herself to the sexual violence [from Guede].'

Mignini said that the 'break-in' had been the key to their defence, 'but it was all simulated.' He added that no blood or DNA evidence from anyone else was found at the crime scene, and nothing of value was stolen. Mignini described Amanda as 'narcissistic, angry, aggressive, manipulative, transgressive, theatrical and easily given to disliking people she disagreed with or who did not follow her ideals... she has a tendency to dominate, be obstructive and in particular we should remember her behaviour in the police station when she was seen doing the splits and cartwheels just after her friend had been murdered.'

Staring at Raffaele, Mignini described him as 'cold, dependent and with a fear of losing the support of others.'

'We must not forget what they are accused of, and the victim – this was a murder accompanied by sexual violence for futile motives,' Mignini continued. 'A 21-year-old girl who a few days later should have gone back to London to see her ill mother who she was close to and who she should have embraced along with her father, sister, and two brothers. But she was not able to return and embrace her family. She was killed in an appalling manner, and the only way they can be with her is at the cemetery. She was literally eliminated.'

As Mignini gave his summation, Amanda appeared distraught at the defence table, particularly when he asked the court to impose life sentences on both defendants if the jury found them guilty. He also called for Amanda to be sentenced to nine months of isolation, or solitary confinement.

When Mignini was finished, Amanda asked if she could address the court and she was given permission to do so. Speaking in near-fluent Italian, as she had done throughout the trial, Amanda began to speak, trying to hold back tears.

'I wanted to speak the other day, but I couldn't,' she said. 'I have to say some important things. This first thing is that Meredith was my friend. I did not hate her. To say that I wanted to take revenge against a person who I liked is absurd. Then I had no relationship with Rudy. Everything that has been said these last two days is pure fantasy. It's not true. I have to insist on this and that's all I want to say. Thank you.'

Amanda's attorney, Ghirga, called Mignini's request for a life sentence and isolation as the type of punishment typically given to a Mafia godfather, part of a harsh punishment known as Rule 41 to prevent a Mafia don from exercising power from within prison walls.

'This request for isolation is one that you would make for different crimes, more associated with Mafia bosses such as Bernardo Provenzano or Toto Riina, not for someone who has a clean record,' Ghirga said. 'She is just a young twenty-something girl. The life sentence was expected, but the request for isolation is too much.'

On Friday, December 4, the jury returned with their verdict. Amanda Knox and Raffaele Sollecito had been found guilty. The jury sentenced Amanda to 26 years in prison, and sentenced Raffaele to 25 years in prison.

Meredith Kercher's brother, Lyle, speaking on behalf of her family at a press conference after the verdicts, said: 'Ultimately we are pleased with the decision, pleased that we've got a decision but it's not a time for celebration.' Arline Kercher also said that she agreed with the court's ruling.

'If the evidence has been presented then, yes, you have to agree with that verdict,' she said. 'It's difficult to say, but at the end of the day you have to go on the evidence because there's nothing else.'

The Kercher family was also awarded 4.4 million euros as compensation, but the family said that it was merely 'symbolic' and that no amount of money could account for the loss they have sustained. Lyle said that the amount awarded was to 'reflect the severity and gravity of the case.'

Meredith's other brother, John, said: 'Everyone in this room associates Meredith with a tragic event, but we would prefer not to remember her in that way. We would like to concentrate on the 21 years that we had with her.'

Others, including the parents of Amanda and Raffaele, considered verdict a travesty of justice. It is widely accepted that appeals are a certainty.

AFTERWORD

Even though Amanda's lawyer, Luciano Ghirga, had commenced with a cutting attack against the prosecution's case, he had broken down in tears during a sometimes poignant closing argument for the defence, as he pleaded for the court to reach a not guilty verdict – the right verdict in his mind – for his client. He had argued, in his own way, that the verdict, whatever it was, would be a reflection on his city, Perugia. In his efforts to sway the jury to his way of thinking, Ghirga had condemned the allegations centred on Amanda's character, even though he had probably known in his heart that a guilty verdict had been headed their way.

'You have the opportunity to make the right decision for our city of Perugia,' he had said. He had also asserted: 'The deductions made about Amanda outside of the courtroom – I don't accept them.'

He had argued, to no avail, that female police officers had 'had it in' for Amanda, perhaps, he had said, 'just because she had condoms and a vibrator in her beauty case' and that his client 'had suffered as a result of this antagonism.'

Co-defence counsel Carlo Della Vedova had said that he was 'stunned' by the attack the prosecution had launched against his client, whom he had characterized as 'just a young girl awaiting justice and she has done so with great courage and determination'. He had also urged the jury to 'not be afraid of errors'.

'The night Amanda was arrested an error was made,' Della Vedova had said. 'You have to have a moral certainty – if you have any doubts then you must clear. Remember here the maximum penalty that was requested is life, with isolation – and we are talking of a young girl just 22 years old.'

Of course, things never turned out the way the defence had hoped, resulting in great disappointment for Amanda, Raffaele, and their families. The airline ticket home to Seattle, purchased for Amanda by her parents expecting her acquittal, would not be used. There had been talk of movies, book deals and media appearances for Amanda upon her return – plans that would no longer be carried out, at least not in the foreseeable future. Amanda's future, as was Raffaele's, was a return to prison, where they would remain pending the outcome of lengthy appeals that most likely would not be heard until autumn 2010. There was also the problem of money, at least for Amanda's appeal. Where would it come from?

Amanda's family has shelled out a reported $1.2 million or more for her defence at trial. Her parents, who are divorced, have taken out additional mortgages on their respective homes, as has her grandmother, to scrape up enough for the trial defence. Her mother and father have stated publicly that they have maxed out their credit cards, and now will probably have to sell their homes in order to continue with Amanda's appeal. With the recent financial crisis that has occurred in America, where homeowners have seen the value of their property plummet, selling their homes may not even be an option at the current time. Edda Mellas recently told reporters that she is seriously considering relocating to Italy, along with her current husband, because that would at least cut out the need for, and expense of, flying back and forth across the Atlantic as they have done for the past two years. But such an option raises the question of how she and her husband would earn money living in a foreign country, and even if they could establish residency and obtain permits to work, it would be questionable if they could earn enough to cover their own expenses *and* the expense of Amanda's appeal. Even if they developed multiple streams of income from self-employment, it seems a daunting challenge awaiting them if they should opt for moving to Italy.

'I'll do whatever it takes for Amanda, however long it takes,' Mellas said after the verdict and sentencing. 'The good news is she will get out of this. The bad news is it could take several more years.'

Nonetheless, Edda Mellas and her family have never given up their belief that Amanda is innocent, nor can any of them even conceive of the possibility that she may have committed a murder, a particularly heinous one at that, despite the evidence, circumstantial that it may be. Mellas believes that Amanda has told the truth throughout the nightmarish ordeal, notwithstanding the fact that she has accused an innocent man of Meredith's murder, which placed her at the crime scene, and later recanted. Would a person who is truly innocent do such a thing?

The jury, however, despite the protestations that a travesty of justice was being committed by even putting her on trial, apparently did not buy the reasoning and excuses put forth by her family and other supporters. They had chosen instead to believe the prosecution's case, the DNA evidence, and Mignini's characterization of Amanda as being 'narcissistic, aggressive, manipulative, transgressive, with a tendency to dominate' and a 'talented and calculating liar.' Mignini was also known to refer to her as 'Luciferina', or the 'She-Devil', which naturally did not sit well with her supporters.

Suddenly, the seven-figure media deals everyone on Amanda's team had hoped for were gone, vanished by the simple word, 'guilty', as if they had never existed. And now Amanda was back in prison, separated from other prisoners for a time as she was being observed by guards at regular 15-minute intervals out of fear that she might decide to take her own life. Later, nine months of isolation or solitary confinement would come. But she was greeted with warm milk and good wishes by other inmates upon her return to Capanne prison after the verdict and sentence had been announced. Despite the *welcome back*, Amanda was said to have cried a lot after her return to the prison.

'Amanda cried for a long time before she eventually got to sleep,' said a source at the prison. 'Sollecito is in the men's section and he was a lot calmer and did not cry like Amanda.'

During his first interview since his conviction for murder, Raffaele Sollecito recently characterized Amanda as 'sweet', and not capable of killing anyone. His interview was published in *Il Messaggero*.

'Amanda is a very dear person to me even if we were only together for a short while. She is also a living nightmare. We both find ourselves in a tremendous situation. I am not in love with Amanda, but I feel close to her as she is my companion in misadventure. Amanda is not capable of killing anyone. It's impossible and absurd. She is such a sweet girl.'

No longer at Capanne prison, Raffaele is now housed in the sex offender's wing at a prison 70 miles north of Rome, where he spends a considerable amount of time praying.

'My faith is what keeps me going,' he said. 'I pray all the time to Padre Pio. I have always been close to my faith, it's not a revelation I have had in these last few terrible months. It's something I have always had. If I didn't have my faith, I would have ended it all.'

He claims he has no idea who murdered Meredith, but said recently that his attorneys have told him that Rudy Guede was the guilty party.

'They showed that in court,' he said. 'I trust them and I can't say anything else because I don't know anything else.'

He said that throughout the ordeal, from the arrest through the prosecution, he had always believed he would be cleared.

'I was certain that the verdict would mean the end of a nightmare, but instead it hasn't been,' he said. 'When they read the sentence out, I didn't understand what was going on. I still don't know. It still seems impossible and I still don't know how I was convicted. The hardest part was when I saw one witness say that he saw me with Rudy, Meredith and Amanda on October 30th.'

His attorney, Luca Maori, said that he is concerned about Raffaele's wellbeing following his conviction and sentence.

'He is suffering psychologically and I am looking at having him transferred somewhere on medical grounds,' Maori said. 'He is innocent of the murder of poor Meredith and he does not understand why he is in jail. When I saw him the after the verdict he was in a state of confusion and kept asking, "Why am I still here?"'

Maori said that Raffaele was continuing with his studies via 'virtual reality' courses at the University of Verona, and that work on his appeal has already begun. Maori is confident that his appeal will be successful and that he will be cleared.

Based on what their lawyers have said, it is believed that both Amanda's and Raffaele's appeal will focus on several key issues, including questions over Amanda's DNA that prosecutors say was found on the handle of the knife and Meredith's DNA found near the blade's tip. They will insist that Amanda's DNA was transferred to the knife while she was cooking, as they have asserted all along, and that Meredith's DNA was an inferior match. Lawyers will argue that the DNA matched to Meredith could belong to half the population of Italy.

The alleged murder weapon will again be called into question during the appeal. Although the prosecution has contended that the kitchen knife found at Raffaele's flat was compatible with Meredith's murder wounds, lawyers will argue – again – that the knife in question failed to match a knife-shaped bloodstain on Meredith's bedclothes. They will also say that its blade did not match two out of the three wounds to her neck.

How the police obtained the knife will also probably be called into question, as it was selected from several found in Raffaele's kitchen because it had looked particularly clean. Its cleanliness, and the fact that a strong smell of bleach was present in the flat, caused *police intuition* to kick in and officers seized the knife because they reasoned it might be of interest. Even though it had been tested for the presence of blood, none had been found on it. If Meredith's DNA found on the knife had not originated from blood, several experts on DNA, including some from the U.S., insist that her DNA most likely came from cross-contamination in the laboratory.

'There exists the real possibility that the low-level partial profile attributed to the knife blade is a result of unintended transfer in the laboratory during sample handling,' one expert wrote.

Another likely point to be visited in the appeal process is the clasp from Meredith's bra found at the scene which investigators said had Raffaele's DNA on it. The rest of the garment had not shown any traces of his DNA even though the police believe that the clasp had been cut from Meredith's bra during the attack. Furthermore, the bra clasp had turned out to be quite controversial, considering how it was collected as evidence.

For example, a police video shot by investigators on November 3, 2007, clearly shows the bra clasp on the floor of Meredith's room, not far from where her body had been found, yet it was not collected as evidence at that time. Instead, it would not be collected as evidence until 45 days later, when police returned to the cottage on December 18, 2007. It was only after it had been collected as evidence that it was tested for DNA, at which time trace amounts of Raffaele's DNA had shown up on it – along with the DNA of three other unidentified people.

'Handling and movement of this sample has compromised its probative value,' said DNA experts in the U.S. 'The laboratory result for this sample cannot reliably be interpreted to show that the DNA of Raffaele Sollecito was actually on the bra clasp at the time of Meredith Kercher's murder, and it does not establish how or when this DNA was deposited or transferred.'

There is also the question of how many killers actually participated in Meredith's murder that will be argued during the appeal process. The prosecution and its witnesses, including forensic pathologists and other forensic experts, contends that more than one person had participated in the murder. They had based their assertions on the size and location of Meredith's injuries and the fact that there was little or no evidence – such as hair or skin found beneath her fingernails – that she had fought back. It is believed that the defence will argue that Amanda did not know Guede well, that perhaps he was only an acquaintance to her, and that Raffaele had not known him at all. Those facts, say the defence, remove credibility from the prosecution premise that the three of them had conspired to kill Meredith. They will insist that only one person committed the murder – Guede, or an unknown person.

The so-called confession and the lies Amanda allegedly told about the night of the murder will also come into play. Why had she accused an innocent man, Patrick Lumumba, and placed herself at the crime scene, hearing Meredith's screams as she was attacked, and later repeated those claims in writing? The defence has indicated that it is prepared to argue that Amanda had spent the night at Raffaele's flat, as she had originally stated, and that her verbal *confession* had been made under duress and should have been inadmissible at trial because she did not have a lawyer present when she provided that version of the evening's events to police.

Defence lawyers would also dispute the mixed DNA between Amanda and Meredith that forensic technicians had found inside the cottage by arguing that it is common to find mixed DNA from two individuals who live together inside the same house.

There are likely to be other points that will be included in the appeals, such as the telephone calls Raffaele purportedly made to the police in an effort to answer the question of whether he had called the police before or after the first officers had arrived at the cottage, and those related to Raffaele's computer.

Amid all of the anger and disbelief expressed by

Amanda's family and other supporters over the convictions and sentences, the arrogance that Americans are so well known for overseas came to a head when Washington State Senator Maria Cantwell came out and publicly called into question the integrity of the Italian justice system, going so far as to suggest that the convictions had been the result of anti-Americanism and vowing to raise her concerns to U.S. Secretary of State Hillary Clinton.

'The prosecution did not present enough evidence for an impartial jury to conclude beyond a reasonable doubt that Miss Knox was guilty,' Cantwell said. 'Italian jurors were allowed to view highly negative news coverage about Miss Knox.'

When word had reached Secretary of State Clinton about Cantwell's concerns relating to the verdict, Clinton was more than happy to get involved and offer her two-cents' worth by agreeing to meet with the senator from Washington.

'Of course I'll meet with Senator Cantwell or anyone who has a concern,' Clinton had said. 'But I can't offer any opinion about that at this time.'

There was even the suggestion at one point that such a *travesty of justice* would not have occurred had Amanda Knox been tried in the U.S. or Britain. The Italians, including Amanda's defence lawyers as well as Prosecutor Mignini, were not at all happy that the government of the U.S. was making such suggestions about the Italian judicial system.

'That's all we need, Hillary Clinton involved,' Luciano Ghirga said. 'I have the same political sympathies as Hillary but this sort of thing does not help us in any way.'

'This senator [Cantwell] should not interfere in something she has no idea about,' Mignini had said. 'I am happy with how the trial went.'

Newspapers printed angry words about the perceived interference or intention to interfere with the Italian justice system by another country, and at least one front-page editorial said that Italy would not 'take lessons from *America*.' Another editorial stated, 'Here we have rule number one for an American accused of a crime abroad – it doesn't matter if they are innocent or guilty. All that counts is their passport.' Another said, 'This same [U.S.] administration can't close Guantanamo, but it can find the time to attack the sentence in Perugia.' Yet another read, 'If there is any ground upon which our country will not be taught lessons on civility and respect from anyone, the United States included, then it is the penal process.'

Meredith's family was not buying the anti-Americanism charges, and said that they believed the defendants had received a fair trial.

'It's ludicrous,' John Kercher said of the anti-Americanism claims. 'I believe the verdict was based entirely on the evidence.'

Despite the support from home, Amanda believes she received a fair trial.

'I have faith in the Italian justice system,' she said after her sentencing. 'I have heard about the reaction in America, and from a human point of view it's appreciated. But it doesn't help me...I'm just waiting for my appeal and I know I will get out sooner or later. I am thinking of Meredith all the time, but I had nothing to do with her murder. I will now have to spend another Christmas in jail away from my family, but hopefully it will be the last one and I will be freed at my appeal. I was able to defend myself in my trial, and my rights were respected.'

The Italian justice system is certainly not a law unto itself, as some articles in the press may have implied. Nobody is 'untouchable' and, in fact, Mignini, the chief prosecutor in the Kercher case, is himself the subject of an inquiry regarding his role as prosecutor in the 'Monster of Florence' court case. Like the murder of Meredith Kercher, this was a very high profile case. So much so that the author of *The Silence of the Lambs*, Thomas Harris, attended and subsequently set much of his book *Hannibal* in Florence. The decision in Mignini's case is due in January 2010.

In the meantime, many people on both sides of the Atlantic are wondering what will become of Amanda Knox. Her father, Curt Knox, recently tried to shed some light on the question.

'She is not going to be left in a foreign prison 6,000 miles away for something she didn't do,' he said. 'It is so crystal clear to me that there is such a huge mistake…and it has to be fixed…soon.'

'None of us will be the same,' chimed in Edda Mellas, 'and Amanda most of all. It's been hard.'

She also offered some words for the Kercher family.

'They lost their child,' Mellas continued. 'There's nothing that compares to that. I can't imagine the pain they are going through for the loss of their child. But we would also tell them that we know absolutely that Amanda had nothing to do with this. Meredith was her friend. And there's a couple of new victims in this whole mess, and that's Amanda and Raffaele.'

Mellas also said that she believes Amanda would be free today if she had left Italy to stay with relatives right after the murder. It would have been incumbent upon prosecutors in Italy to show that there was enough evidence against her to justify extraditing her back to Italy.

'I kick myself everyday that I didn't make her leave the country, and so does my cousin in Germany,' she added. 'Because, had she left, none of this would've happened. She wouldn't be where she's at. But, you know, we can't go back and fix that – we just need to go forward…they'll get it right in appeals, she will get out of there. They will not…put away this innocent young girl for a crime she didn't commit. Her lawyers have told her to have courage.'

In the meantime, the Kerchers know that nothing will bring Meredith back to them. Arline Kercher said that she has kept Meredith's room precisely the way it was when she was still alive.

'It's still Mez's room,' Arline Kercher said. 'It has barely been touched, but it is a constant reminder of her. When I am walking past with a pile of washing in my hand I get a feeling of sadness. It is almost as if she has gone out for a while and she will be back – but she won't.'

She also said that family members have ruled out moving away from the family home.

'That's my way of handling it,' she said. 'If we moved she wouldn't know where I am. It's silly, really. We will carry Meredith around with us all the time…we are the ones who have been given a life sentence. We have been living a nightmare for two years. People say that time heals, but it doesn't.'